Praise for
Great CEOs Are Lazy

"*Great CEOs Are Lazy* is a brilliant book for anyone who wants to win as an entrepreneur or CEO. Schleckser's insights are powerful and practical—ripe for growth-oriented CEOs wanting to get to the top and be happy."
—Tom Adams, former CEO of Rosetta Stone, chairman of Pedago, and Ernst & Young's National Entrepreneur of the Year winner (2009)

"Do you work seven days a week and still feel you're not doing enough? *Great CEOs Are Lazy* will show you how to focus your time on things that really matter to grow your unique company—and improve your lifestyle at the same time!"
—Richard G. Stieglitz, PhD, author of *Leadership Conversations*, former CEO of RGS Associates

"Jim Schleckser taught me many years ago that to be a great CEO I needed to focus all of my energy on relieving the top bottlenecks in my business, one at a time. I learned that great CEOs did not spread themselves around 'like peanut butter' trying to touch everyone in the organization. Instead, a great CEO has the discipline and guts to relentlessly attack the bottleneck until it is removed. Then he or she moves to the next bottleneck."
—Dave Lindsey, founder & chairman, DEFENDERS

"Jim Schleckser shares the secrets of how great CEOs elevate their leadership game and guide their business's performance to the next level. He reveals that great CEOs are lazy—like a fox—in strategically working *on* the business versus getting lost *in* it."
—Jim Haudan, CEO of Root Learning, author of *The Art of Engagement*

"Dense with information, Schleckser uses great real-life examples and stories to illustrate how great leaders have applied the Lazy CEO principles to improve themselves and their businesses."
—Dave Hood, CEO of The Original Cakerie

"I was hooked after the first chapter. I like to say CEOs don't really do anything—they just cause things to happen and remove obstacles. Jim does an excellent job of describing just how being 'lazy' will make you a better CEO. He doesn't just offer theoretical advice, he gives you practical examples and strategies on how to become a more effective and lazy CEO."
—Maria Haggerty, CEO of Dotcom Distribution

"Jim Schleckser has boiled the secrets of great CEOs down to *focus* and *leverage* and dives deep on each of these areas to show you how the best CEOs perform at such a high level."
—Phil Nolan, CEO of Camber Corporation, former CEO of Stanley Associates

"How do exceptional CEOs get more done in less time than everyone else? How do they add great value to the business—and still have time for family, friends, and personal passions? *Great CEOs Are Lazy* shows you how they do it."
—Tom Searcy, founder & CEO of Hunt Big Sales

"Jim Schleckser's insights, culled from thousands of real world interviews with top CEOs, have freed me to minimize time spent in the business, with maximum impact. I have used the concepts of *focus* and *leverage* as well as the Five Hats to improve my business and still live a balanced life.
—Neal Rothermel, CEO of VMS Biomarketing

GREAT CEOs ARE LAZY

GREAT CEOs ARE LAZY

HOW EXCEPTIONAL CEOS DO MORE IN LESS TIME

JIM SCHLECKSER

AN INC. ORIGINAL

Published by An Inc. Original Imprint, Mansueto Ventures
7 World Trade Center
New York, NY 10007

Copyright © 2016 by Jim Schleckser

All rights reserved.

No part of this book may be reproduced, scanned, or distributed in any printed or electronic form without written permission from the copyright holder or a stated representative. To get permission for authorized use, contact info@IncCEOProject.com.

Cover design by Sheila Parr
Book design by Alex Head, Draft Lab LLC
Cover image: © Ditty_about_summer/Shutterstock.com

ISBN: 978-0-9883099-1-3

Printed in the United States of America
16 17 18 19 20   10 9 8 7 6 5 4 3 2
First edition

Dedicated to my father, Henry Schleckser

CONTENTS

Introduction 1

Chapter One: Identifying Your Point of Constraint 5

Chapter Two: The Learner Hat 31

Chapter Three: The Architect Hat 57

Chapter Four: The Coach Hat 93

Chapter Five: The Engineer Hat 131

Chapter Six: The Player Hat 159

Conclusion 177

Acknowledgments 181

Index 183

About the Author 193

INTRODUCTION

I choose a lazy person to do a hard job. Because a lazy person will find an easy way to do it.
—Bill Gates

There really is nothing comparable to being the leader of a company. It is probably the hardest job in any organization. As the leader of your organization—the person to whom everyone else looks for direction, inspiration, confidence, support, and more—you face no shortage of demands on your time. As soon as you put out one fire, another pops up. That's particularly true when you're in start-up mode, when you're likely trying to do everything from closing the books and sweeping the floors to making sales and sending out invoices. But attending to all aspects of running your organization isn't sustainable. As your business grows, the number of hours you work will increase until you need to hire new employees to lessen your workload. You will need to continually upgrade and improve how you work as long as your company is expanding. If you stop growing, your business will stop growing.

The Inc. CEO Project is a firm dedicated to helping high-performance CEOs grow their businesses. After learning firsthand the lessons of running a company, we have turned these experiences into tools to help business leaders reap the benefits of the successes and learn from the failures of others.

By conducting more than a thousand in-depth interviews with CEOs over a seven-year period and counting, we developed insights about what exceptional CEOs do differently from CEOs whose companies do OK or simply don't perform at all. In these interviews, which averaged forty minutes, we dug into their business models, strategic positioning, talent, business processes, how they learned, and what tasks they spent most of their time on.

Just about every CEO we spoke with was leading a growing organization and most had been recognized for their success by organizations like *Inc.* magazine, *Businessweek*, and *Forbes,* or they had won awards such as the Deloitte Fast 50 or the Ernst & Young Entrepreneur of the Year. Every leader was acknowledged as a high performer in their field, yet they didn't achieve uniformly high results.

We learned that the most gifted and productive CEOs think about their businesses and their roles differently from their more "average" peers. They view themselves and their businesses far more systematically. What shocked us was that the best CEOs' secret to achieving extreme performance was to be "strategically lazy." You're probably wondering how CEOs can be both great *and* lazy, right?

Great CEOs are *very clear* about working hard on *a very limited number of tasks* that make all the difference to their businesses, and they refuse to spend significant time on anything else. These CEOs understand that when it comes to growing a company, a specific set of activities and roles will get them the most bang for their buck. If you ask them to do anything else, you will find a profoundly lazy person.

And just what are these activities and roles they thrive at? In a nutshell, Lazy CEOs recognize that they need to make hard choices about where and what to spend their time on in their business. They use the theory of constraints to identify where they should spend time. We call their Lazy CEO approach to engaging the point of constraint wearing "the five hats": the Learner hat, the Architect hat, the Coach hat, the Engineer hat, and the Player hat. These are the leveraged roles that enable a leader to make an investment in creating organizational assets that pay back over time. More important, the improvements are sustainable without continued involvement by the leader. Leverage is not about the short-term impact. Leverage is about the permanent improvement in organizational capacity to execute.

In the following pages, you'll learn how to identify the point of constraint in your business and "try on" the hats and learn more about when to use each and why. We'll begin by sharing some of the tools and techniques any CEO can use to identify the constraints in his or her business and then assess which hat to put on to tackle them. We will then examine each of the hats to understand how they work and when to use them. We have seen hundreds of CEOs apply these ideas and transform themselves into Lazy CEOs who get amazing business results.

Chapter One
IDENTIFYING YOUR POINT OF CONSTRAINT

Every action that does not bring the company closer to its goal is not productive.
—Eliyahu Goldratt

One night a man walking down a street turns a corner and sees another man, down on his hands and knees on the sidewalk, under a streetlight, clearly trying to find something. "Hey buddy," the Good Samaritan says. "What are you looking for?"

The second man stumbles a bit as he answers. "I'm looking for my keys," he says. "I really need to get home." It's obvious he's had a few drinks.

"OK," the first man says, "I'll help you."

After searching for fifteen minutes, the keys are still nowhere to be found. "Where exactly were you when you lost them?" the helpful stranger asks.

"Over there in that dark alley."

Stunned, the first guy says, "Well then, why are we looking out here on the sidewalk?"

"Because the light is better," says our drunken friend.

If you can forgive the old joke, there is actually an important lesson to be learned here: Lots of leaders and CEOs spend their time where it's light, where they're comfortable, while the real problems lurk in the dark alleys they don't want to venture into. They get stuck working hard in low-leverage roles. To drive organizational performance to new levels, leaders need to be willing to stretch themselves beyond their comfort zones and challenge themselves to tackle tasks that will truly lead to results.

A CEO'S PRIMARY MISSION

If you wanted to water plants in your garden and you squeezed the handle on the hose nozzle and the water only dribbled out, you'd quickly realize that a kink in the hose was restricting the flow. Solving the problem, of course, would be as simple as locating and untangling the kink. What would happen if you began to think about your company's flow rate—the revenues, profits, growth, and service to your customers—in the same way? If you find yourself confronting poor results—a dribble—or even if you are looking for new paths for growth in your company's performance, wouldn't your time be best served identifying and removing the kinks? Unfortunately, many executives try to get more water to flow without dealing with the underlying issue—the kink in the hose.

To drive organizational performance to new levels, leaders need to be willing to stretch themselves beyond their comfort zones and challenge themselves to tackle tasks that will truly lead to results.

Obviously every business is far more complex than a garden hose is. But the lesson about identifying and removing constraints—anything that prevents you from reaching your goals—holds true. This notion was studied extensively by Eliyahu Goldratt, an Israeli physicist turned management guru who defined the Theory of Constraints, which can be summed up by the ancient adage that no chain is stronger than its weakest link. Goldratt believed that the very best organizations learn to continually identify their weakest links and then restructure to remove these links in a way that could propel the organization forward—unkinking the hose. Most important, all work that is not at the point of constraint is a waste. Yet, thousands of CEOs continue to work all along the hose, hoping that some of their effort is actually useful rather than finding the kink and applying all of their time and effort at that point.

In his research, Goldratt focused most of his early work on manufacturing operations and, specifically within that realm, on finding what one process or piece of equipment might be inhibiting throughput. But the same principles apply regardless of the system or process you study. Your primary mission as CEO is to identify and remove constraints, whether they're related to quickly designing new products; understanding why you're not fulfilling orders fast enough; figuring out why it takes so long to hire people, close the books, or acquire new customers; or determining why you can't keep your customers coming back. Do these sound like tasks a CEO should delegate? Do you think you should be spending more time focusing on things that don't add as much organizational value?

> All work that is not at the point of constraint is a waste.

Not based on our research. The point is that the single most important job any CEO of a growing company can perform is identifying the constraints that are keeping the organization from sprinting forward in the right direction and then allocating as much of their time as needed to remove them, thus freeing up space for the organization to perform more effectively. Using the garden hose analogy, our Lazy CEO will notice the dribble of water, find the kink in the hose, untangle it, promptly hand the hose back to someone in the organization, make sure the system won't allow another kink at that place, and eventually head back to their lounge chair. After all, you can't harvest the fruits of your labor if your garden dies from a lack of water.

THE ERROR OF UNIFORM TIME ALLOCATION

A lot of the mediocre and hardworking CEOs we have run into over the years are exceptionally good at what we call "peanut buttering." When it comes to allocating their time to the various tasks and stakeholders in their businesses—their boards, their supply chains, their investors, their communities, etc.—these CEOs do their best to spread their time as evenly as possible across all of them. The concern, of course, is to make sure everyone feels like they're getting the CEO's attention. In this effort, the CEO will work very hard, sometimes as much as eighty or more hours a week. The bad news is that this is the surest way possible to dilute the CEO's impact on any one issue. Unfortunately, this concept of tending to every stakeholder is taught at many major business schools, which only perpetuates the error. This is done, in part, because CEOs aren't certain what actions will drive the business forward; consequently, they work on all fronts, hoping one will yield results.

Lazy CEOs, on the other hand, play favorites with their time. Rather than allocating a uniform amount of time to everyone and everything, they give usually between 30 and 50 percent of their time specifically to the task of removing the constraint(s) in the business. Remember this: It's only the work done at the point of the kink in the hose—the constraint—that will truly make a difference in your business. Whatever time is left gets distributed to the other stakeholders—some of whom may get zero CEO attention then, or perhaps forever. In an ideal world, smart CEOs would build a strong organization of individuals who would handle all of the work that is not at the point of constraint. That way, the only work our Lazy CEO would do would be to remove each constraint as it arises.

Unfortunately, since a business is a complex system, the diagnostic phase of identifying the true constraint, the root cause, is not an easy task. Let's say, for example, that a business is unable to fulfill orders on time. This kind of issue can have a ripple impact throughout the organization, affecting everyone from customers to suppliers. It will show up as a slower growth rate, reduced margins, or even customer losses.

> It's only the work done at the point of the kink in the hose—the constraint—that will truly make a difference in your business.

But think about the difference between a CEO spending 10 percent of his time on that issue versus the CEO who dedicates 50 percent of her time to it. That second CEO will remove the constraint five times faster—and thus allow the company to move forward more quickly—than her mediocre counterpart who remains committed to peanut buttering his time. With the constraint having been cleared more quickly, the CEO can concentrate on removing the next impediment. When you can carry this out over time, the compound impact is profound. Given that most CEOs don't even know where the constraint lies in their organization, it is easy to see how exceptional CEOs generate results many times better than unfocused CEOs do.

==Dealing with a constraint is a two-step process: First, you have to go on the diagnostic journey to identify it, and second, you need to make the time to implement the therapy to solve it.== This effort of focusing on identifying and removing constraints is relevant only for companies that have a stated objective, whether it be generating improved growth and greater profitability, increasing cash flow, servicing more clients, or increasing market share or position. We will delve into how to assess your business later in this chapter.

Quantitatively measuring such objectives is critical to determining if progress is being made. The point is, if you know where you want to go, and you can identify what's keeping your organization from getting there, you can then spend the time you need to correct that issue. If you're happy running a lifestyle business, for instance, you probably don't face any true constraints on where you want the business to go, although there is the question of optimizing how little time one can spend in the business and still get acceptable results.

> Given that most CEOs don't even know where the constraint lies in their organization, it is easy to see how exceptional CEOs generate results many times better than unfocused CEOs do.

In our experience working with Inc. 500/5000 companies—the fastest-growing companies in the country—we've dealt with constraints that come in many different forms. And, interestingly enough, we've found in working with the CEOs of these companies that about half of them already know what the big constraint in their organization is. That's right; roughly 50 percent *know* the thing that is holding back their company. Unfortunately, this also means that half of the CEOs *do not know* or understand their point of constraint. This is clearly a problem. You might ask yourself which half you are in.

CONSTRAINTS ARE CONTROLLABLE

It's important to identify constraints that are within your control. It's not productive, for example, to blame climate change, the state of the economy, or the president of the United States for the stagnation of your business. You can't change any of those factors. Let me give you an example to illustrate how realizing this led one CEO to recognize the true kink in the company's hose.

Inc. CEO Project worked with a service company a few years ago that dealt with repairs to high-voltage electricity wires. The barely profitable business was struggling to remain afloat, but it always flourished when hurricanes and ice storms hit because those natural disasters usually meant lots of extra work at overtime rates to help repair downed power lines for power companies. The CEO had no control over the weather, so he could hardly fault it as the point of constraint for his company. While he could pray for a hurricane, he had other issues he needed to address, like the fact that his business model was so dependent on bad weather for its success.

In essence, what we're looking for are areas where you, the CEO, can step in and make a difference by serving in one of the five high-leverage roles—putting on one of the five hats—that all Lazy CEOs deploy: Learner, Architect, Coach, Engineer, and Player. Let's quickly go through the five hats.

The Learner: Great CEOs realize that they don't have all of the answers, and they likewise realize that to keep their company growing, they have to keep learning. They are curious. This means finding ways to educate yourself both inside and outside your organization. When you put your Learner hat on, you gain the ability to integrate your prior experience with your new situation and to see over the hill and gauge what's coming next in terms of informing and sparking the kinds of new ideas that will continue to propel your business.

The Architect: When you're wearing the Architect hat, you're spending time improving your existing business model or taking a new business concept and building up the elements to support it. You're planning, thinking, and plotting strategy. Every hour you invest will yield a strong multiplier effect, a disproportionate return. The goal is to build a superior business model with high margins, a compelling offer, low capital needs, and good recurring revenue because this type of business is easier to grow, operate, and, potentially, sell.

The Coach: With your Coach hat on (and maybe an optional whistle in your hand), you'll spend your time thinking about employee talent: how to acquire it, improve it, and divest yourself of underperforming team members.

The Engineer: When you're wearing the Engineer hat, you're working on implementing and improving the processes that align with the value proposition of your business along with the measurement systems to check your progress. With your Architect hat on you ask, "What?" With your Engineer hat on you ask, "How?" You're thinking about how to create that "Wow!" experience for your customers. In other words, you're looking for ways to make functional and systematic improvements to your organization.

The Player: When great CEOs put on the Player hat, they dip into the company's different functional areas such as sales, marketing, product design, accounting, operations, or whatever their particular gifts or passions might be. Wearing your Player hat from time to time can be a valuable use of your time, particularly when it allows you to keep in touch with your business. In other words, by wearing the Player hat, you can help identify opportunities to tackle when you're wearing the other hats.

The five hats are a useful mnemonic to remember the roles you should be playing at any given time. They can also be used to determine if a particular task is high leverage (one of the hats) or is something that is more appropriately delegated. But the question is, what hat should you wear at what point? This is where we need to delve into assessing your business in pursuit of the kink in the hose.

ASSESSING YOUR BUSINESS

As the popular saying goes, "If you can't measure it, you can't improve it." If you don't yet know what your constraint is, it probably means you do not have the proper metrics in your business to give you direction.

DON'T KNOW WHERE TO START (LEARNER HAT)?

Metrics that track each process important to customers should help point to the kink in your hose. A great question to ask yourself is this: "If I came upon a genie and he granted me a single wish to make my business better, what would I change?" Get a quicker close cycle? Faster service delivery? An improved ability to attract excellent talent? Chances are, whatever you settled on is likely a good place to start looking for your constraint.

If you do not have measurements deployed in your business that help point to the constraint, then ask the following questions:

1. What's the one area in your business where a change could bring about the most profound economic (revenue or profitability) impact?

2. What's the biggest risk factor your business faces? What one thing could derail your business? For example, is there a key customer relationship that your business may be too highly leveraged against such that if you lost them, you might lose your business as well?

3. What's your organization's biggest pain point (i.e., the one issue or difficulty that persistently remains unresolved)? This could be something that impacts internal operations or clients.

One of the goals in performing this kind of assessment is to help determine in what area of the business you should be spending the bulk of your time. To put that another way, you're trying to find the kink that will help inform which of the hats you should be wearing most of your time. This is why it is also useful to begin to look more deeply at more specific indicators within your business that might clue you into the kind of work you should be focusing on. To do that, you almost need to start thinking like a doctor or an investigator in learning to ask the kinds of questions and to identify the sorts of clues that will help uncover what's really holding up the growth of your business.

Inevitably, operating with the Learner hat on your head to determine what is next or to find the kink in the hose is high-leverage work. A fair amount of your effort should be focused inside the business, looking at metrics, delving into talent and processes; a fair amount of your effort should be outside the business too, looking for some breakthrough thinking. We will cover the Learner hat in depth in chapter two.

> **Areas to Focus On**
> - Track each process using metrics.
> - Ask in which area of your business a change would yield the biggest impact.
> - Ask what's the biggest risk factor your company faces.
> - Ask what your organization's biggest pain point is.

DO YOU HAVE BUSINESS MODEL PROBLEMS (ARCHITECT HAT)?
The very first business I worked in made a reinforced plastic material, one of the original plastics invented by Leon Baekeland in 1907. There were lots of smart people, millions of dollars' worth of physical plant and equipment, and rigorous processes, yet we had a hard time

growing. In a good year, this business could generate a 4–5 percent growth rate year over year—basically GDP growth plus some price increases. The number of customers we added each year matched the number of customers we lost. It was a moribund environment, which ultimately led to my departure. When I look back at that company, I now recognize that they had a significant business model problem.

Lack of Momentum

The first clue that a business model problem exists is a sense that the business lacks momentum in some way, like my first business. That's opposed to feeling like the organization is "winning" and there's a lot of upside still left to take advantage of. When you have a flaw in your business model, it can feel like you're stuck in the mud and there's no easy way to get the wheels moving again. If you feel like you're working hard and smart and still not seeing any progress, that's a sure sign you're dealing with a business model problem.

The best businesses, on the other hand, have developed an incredibly compelling offer. Something that makes customers take notice and allows the business to consistently win new clients. The primary issue is getting in front of potential clients, because if they understand, they'll buy. Goldratt called this a "Mafia Offer," that is, an offer you can't refuse. (You'll read much more on this concept in chapter three.)

Capital Intensity

Another important clue that your business model has flaws is if the business is constantly short of cash or needs a cash infusion every time there is an opportunity to grow. Consider the case of a steel distribution company we worked with. Rather than making the steel, which was highly engineered and used in the oil and gas industry, they bought it on speculation and then custom finished it based on the customer's order. It was a highly capital-intensive business that required $0.50 of capital for every dollar of revenue growth in the business. Unfortunately, it wasn't a high-margin business and thus couldn't fund its own growth. That meant that every time the business landed a new significant contract, they would have to go out and borrow money from banks in order to afford the steel inventory they would need to support their customers. The result was that the business was constantly digging deeper into debt.

The question for the CEO was this: Is this really valuable growth; are we increasing the value of the enterprise? The company began selling equity in the business to get the capital they needed to keep growing. This is always an option of last resort, as the business would have been better off finding ways to reengineer its supply chain and customers in some way that allowed them to grow without needing as much capital. They ultimately accomplished this and materially reduced the cash use and cash per dollar of revenue required—and best of all, they needed a lot fewer trips to the bank to fund growth!

Low Gross Margin

Another clue that you're dealing with a flawed business model is that your gross margins are too tight—say, anything less than 30 percent. If you're dealing with tight margins like that, you almost certainly can't grow rapidly without an infusion of outside cash. The steel company we discussed fell into this category as well. They simply couldn't generate enough profit to fuel their own growth.

Low Profitability

A related measure is looking at how profitable you are relative to sales. If your profits are anything less than 10 percent of your sales, your growth will likely be constrained in a significant way and you are certainly not rewarding your shareholders for the risks involved in owning a business. It's not efficient when you have to raise outside money every time you want to grow. Plus, with limited returns, finding investors will be difficult. Clearly, the benefit of having a highly profitable business is that you can generate the kind of cash that fuels your growth without having to access outside debt or equity capital.

Low Recurring Revenue

Another symptom of a flawed business model is a lack of recurring revenue, which typically results from subscriptions or long-term contracts with your customers. Think about what it would be like to run a construction firm. You land a single job at a time with no guarantee that you'll land another after you're done. The key question to ask yourself on January 1 is, how much revenue am I guaranteed this year? The answer is your real recurring revenue number. Of course, the higher the number, the better off you are. In the case of our construction company, the answer could very easily be zero or, at best, perhaps a few months of revenue in backlog once they finish the existing projects. It is extremely difficult to grow a business like this, let alone finance it and ultimately sell it. We discuss recurring revenue in more depth in chapter three.

> Another symptom of a flawed business model is a lack of recurring revenue.

Low Return on Capital Employed

A final symptom for you to consider when it comes to analyzing the health of your business model is to assess the rate of return on the risk-adjusted cost of your capital. Businesses destroy capital in many hidden ways, and this is one approach to uncover one of the most common and most commonly misunderstood ways it happens. It is important to determine if you are delivering at least an adequate return on the capital you are employing in your business. For an investment to be worthwhile, the expected return on capital—both debt and equity to the cash used—must be greater than the cost of capital. The cost of capital is the rate of return that capital could be expected to earn in an alternative investment of equivalent risk.

Let's say, for example, that your cost of capital is 10 percent. That would mean that an investor might expect to make 15 percent or higher on their investment in your company due to the risk inherent in that investment. If the return on capital rate for your business is anything less than 15 percent, your business is essentially destroying wealth. In other words, your business might be making some money, but it might be doing so while also destroying capital in the process because there are better investments for that level of risk. If this is the case, then it is a serious red flag indicating that you need to rework your business plan.

What happens in many businesses is that the areas that are performing well can obscure a poorly performing area. A single line could be destroying wealth while the other lines cover for it. But when you can both identify the poor-performing unit and correct it, perhaps by exiting that business, you can create a ripple effect from which the entire organization benefits. Sometimes stopping something can be as powerful as starting something because it allows you to focus.

Areas to Target
- Lack of momentum—a growth rate under 5 percent
- Capital intensity ($0.50 or more capital/$1.00 of sales)
- Low gross margin (under 30 percent)
- Low profitability (under 10 percent)
- Low recurring revenue (anything below 50 percent)
- Low return on capital employed (under cost of capital)

DO YOU HAVE PROBLEMS WITH YOUR EMPLOYEE TALENT (COACH HAT)?

A CEO has many opportunities to play the role of Coach with individual performers and teams—something we'll talk more about in chapter four. But one clear indicator that you might have *a talent problem* on your hands is if you find yourself repeatedly swooping in more and more often doing *someone else's* job. You do it because you're good at that task, and you figure you're helping out the other key employee as well as the company. But you could be overlooking a key constraint in your business.

You Are Covering for a Low-Performing Employee

In one company we worked with, a food exporter, the CEO found himself involved with closing the books on a monthly basis because he would regularly uncover errors made by the CFO. When we asked the CEO about such poor performance, he insisted that the CFO was doing a great job but needed a hand during crunch time. While the CEO's loyalty was admirable, he nevertheless needed to replace the CFO so he could free up his time for higher-value work. This CEO wasn't being lazy enough. Rather, he was beginning to tolerate a situation in which he had to continuously do his CFO's job. He ultimately replaced the CFO, and once the right person was in place, the CEO didn't need to be involved in closing the books again.

You Wouldn't Rehire the Employee

When you consistently find an individual who is performing poorly, that's a key sign you have a talent problem. The symptoms of poor performance are subtler when it comes to your B players, those folks who aren't your superstars but who still serve valuable functions on the team. You'll need to look deeper and more regularly to track if they are performing well compared to your A players, whose high-profile work shines a bright light on the B players' successes and failures alike. Ask yourself: "Would I rehire this person if he were to leave and then ask to come back?" For a C player the answer is no. For a B, the answer is yes. In the case of an A, you'd work hard to make sure he or she never left you in the first place.

Your Team Doesn't Have a Commitment to Learning

You should also observe how transparent and open to learning your team members are. If you start seeing a pattern where some people are defensive about being coached or accepting feedback—by implying that their work is perfect or that they have done the job as well as anyone else could—then you know you have a significant issue to deal with. Negative attitudes like this can be poisonous if they're allowed to exist in the organization.

An Employee Isn't Committed to Team Performance

You'll also likely see a lack of alignment with these defensive and negative folks in terms of how their performance stacks up with their team. They may be working on their own agenda instead, which leads to missed execution and poor performance.

As CEO, you'll need to assess if you need to step in as Coach in these circumstances or remedy the situation by replacing the person altogether. One thing you can't afford to do is nothing; action is needed if an employee is at the point of being a constraint. If you decide to live with bad behavior, you'll undermine the sense of trust among the team and its ability to work in a collaborative way. Ultimately, you will lose the team's confidence in your leadership as well. That's when team performance really suffers.

Ideas and Energy Don't Bubble Up to You

Ask yourself about the energy and idea flow between you and your direct reports: Do your people generate as many exciting ideas about the business as you do? Is there a lot of energy that bubbles up and helps feed you as you map out the future of the organization? Or do you find that you're the one supplying all the ideas and energy to those who report to you? It's simply not sustainable for you to be the one injecting all of your energy to help your team amp up their game. Eventually, that won't scale, and you'll be out of energy, ideas, and, ultimately, luck.

> **Areas to Examine**
> - You are covering for a low-performing employee.
> - You wouldn't rehire the employee.
> - Your team doesn't have a commitment to learning.
> - An employee isn't committed to team performance.
> - Ideas and energy don't bubble up to you.

DO YOU HAVE SYSTEMS AND PROCESSES PROBLEMS (ENGINEER HAT)?

When it comes to running your high-performance business, have you found it necessary to bring aboard more and more employees to make things work, without the advantages of your scale? If so, it's likely that you have some glaring holes and weaknesses in your systems and processes.

Recurring Need to Hire Superstars

It's unrealistic and unsustainable to expect that you will be able to tap a steady stream of superstars capable of driving your organization forward. You hear this in sales all of the time, when a CEO complains that he has a talent problem because he can't find the right person to head up the sales team or be a salesperson. But is it possible that rather than a talent problem, the company is really facing the fact that they haven't created the kinds of systems that allow ordinary people to perform in extraordinary ways? In other words, they haven't done the marketing job of developing the business offer and value proposition and connecting them to their clients. In the early days, the business will be talent led, but as it grows and scales, robust processes are needed.

Think about McDonald's. While they would love to recruit superstars to fill out the rosters of all of their restaurants, the truth is they count on motivationally challenged teenagers to deliver fast food to their customers. McDonald's needs robust systems and training to turn those teenagers into a fast food symphony so that the dining experience will be remarkably similar at all of their restaurants around the world. That's the power of having great processes and systems.

Missed Commitments

Another symptom that indicates problematic system issues is that your organization is having trouble meeting its commitments—in terms of production, if you are a product company, or even in closing sales. Maybe your product development team has begun to have trouble predicting release times for your new products. Or the problem could show up in the back office, where you find that closing the books has begun taking longer. Because predictable timeliness is a symptom of high-quality processes, all three of these situations are examples of opportunities to improve by reengineering your processes and systems in a way that increases speed and efficiency without having to re-staff the organization with superstars.

The Seven Wastes

Increased waste throughout the organization is another sign that you have room to improve your processes. Take Toyota, for instance. Through its Toyota Production System (TPS), the company tracks waste in seven categories that fall under the acronym TIMWOOD: Time, Inventory, Motion, Waiting, Over-Processing, Over-Production, and Defects. If you find that your people are constantly forced to redo work or that people are waiting around for another task to finish before they can begin, you likely have a process problem that you should correct as soon as possible. While this TPS model was developed for manufacturing, it can also be applied to administrative systems and professional service businesses. (See chapter five for more details on TPS.)

Improving Cycle Time

Speed is a competitive advantage. There is a phrase that goes, "The large don't eat the small; the quick eat the slow." Imagine a product development time that took half as long, or a delivery process that could get product to customer in one day instead of two weeks. Both of these are potentially sources of competitive advantage. Perhaps even more exciting is developing an offer and a customer base that paid before the product was delivered rather than ninety days after delivery!

Alignment with Strategic Advantage

You should also be thinking about what your competitive advantage is when it comes to your customers and how your systems and processes help strengthen your position—or weaken it. The goal is to create happy customers who feel they are getting good value so they will buy more and refer you to others.

You should also look at how aligned your current systems and processes are in terms of what your target customers value the most. While you may have invested in that brand-new accounting system, your customers might still be frustrated by how slowly you are getting your product to them. It's not that a new accounting system won't help; it's just that it needs to be good enough for you to get the job done. But where you really want to invest your precious time and resources is in those processes that will drive how your customers think about your products, services, and value. Be careful here, because different customers value different things. If you try to create an acceptable offer for all of the potential clients, you will never be excellent at serving any one set of them. You have to pick which clients are most important and optimize for them.

> **Areas to Focus On**
> - Recurring need to hire superstars
> - Missing commitments—unpredictable timeliness
> - Eliminating the seven wastes—TIMWOOD
> - Improving cycle time—speed wins
> - Aligning processes with strategic advantage

DO YOU HAVE TO DIVE IN AND HELP (PLAYER HAT)?

The CEO is usually a very strong individual performer as well as being the leader of the business. And there is nothing like the impact a CEO can provide to a project or a special effort. Unfortunately, this strength can be overused and become a weakness.

Need to Help a Team

At times a team with an important project needs some help, be it a capacity issue or help clearing roadblocks. Lazy CEOs will sometimes jump into a project and help a team get it finished. Many times, this is a sales project where the CEO title helps make the customer comfortable and closes the sale. Almost all CEOs will do this, but Lazy CEOs go one step further and ask why they were needed; and they make moves to prevent it from happening again.

Time to Set an Example

The CEO owns the standard for performance, and as we alluded to previously, you will get what you tolerate. When the organization needs an example of what the standard looks like, usually because they are not performing, a Lazy CEO will show them. Once again, your example is important, but the real benefits are the changes that will allow the team to hold to the standard. Otherwise, you'll be back in to show them the right level of performance again and again.

Need to Cover for Someone You Terminated

I once had a VP of Sales who was simply not performing as a leader, but he was an excellent individual contributor. After working to help him see this and change, I ultimately terminated him—leaving myself without a VP of Sales. This meant that I had to take over the role until I could figure out the best way to proceed. The clarity I gained from a few months in the job allowed me to make a much better decision and ultimately elevate two regional managers and split the Country. Taking the job was only temporary and made for a better call on the new approach.

The Best Way to Learn

You can see a pattern here. Lazy CEOs will go into Player mode, but only to learn and understand the point of constraint. They start with the end in mind, which is to back out of Player mode, deploying talent and systems to improve the organization permanently. Bad CEOs get stuck in Player mode and cannot seem to get out.

> **Areas to Focus On**
> - Need to help a team
> - Time to set an example
> - Need to cover for someone you terminated
> - Use Player mode to learn

WHERE TO START?

As a Lazy CEO who alternately wears an Architect hat, a Coach hat, and an Engineer hat, you ask yourself these types of questions on a regular basis. That's how you'll be able to constantly keep on top of identifying and removing your constraints. But what happens if you identify more than one constraint at any given time? How do you determine which one to tackle first?

The best place to start is to make a list of all of the primary constraints you've identified and then assign an economic value to each one based on how much it could impact the business. Again, it all relates to the objective you have for your organization. Issues surrounding profitability may not be as important as those related to growth, for instance, or perhaps you're most concerned with building as much strategic protection around your business model as possible.

> As CEOs seek to understand the point of constraint, the Learner hat is almost always the first hat they put on in any cycle of improvement.

Once you've got your list and sorted it in order of value, it's time to reallocate your own time and find which of the five hats fits best with the task. Interestingly, as CEOs seek to understand the point of constraint, the Learner hat is almost always the first hat they put on in any cycle of improvement. You will too. Thereafter, if you have a business model issue, it's time to pull your Architect hat off the shelf. Is talent your problem? Then the Coach hat is your answer. If you have a serious systems issue, it's time to start thinking like an Engineer. And sometimes you might have to dig in as a Player to directly impact the situation, with your goal being to learn enough to deploy talent and systems even as you exit Player mode.

If you have multiple constraints it may be tempting to go after some or all of them at once. This is a mistake. You need to focus on the first item on your list until you've eliminated it. Once you've knocked off the first item, take another look at your constraints and re-rank the items—their potential impact may have shifted once you solved the first constraint. If your top priority was correcting your customer acquisition process, for example, you may find that your revenue has suddenly spiked, which means that your new top issue becomes how you're adding the capacity that you need to support production.

The first issue that should get attention is any risk to the business that could end the business. Perhaps you have a sole supplier that is in financial straits, or your relationship is weakening with a customer that accounts for 70 percent of your revenue. Once that risk factor is resolved or mitigated, move to the biggest economic impact, be it constraint or opportunity. In the case of a tie, where you really can't determine which constraint is holding back your company the most, we recommend that you use this order of attack:

1. Wear the *Learner* hat to dig in and understand the business while you are on the diagnostic journey to find the point of constraint.

2. Go into *Architect* mode to fix your business model. If you get this right, everything else becomes much easier.

3. Tackle your employee talent issues as *Coach*. Your business model trumps talent because it won't do you any good to focus on hiring great people until you know exactly what you need them to do. Hiring the very best multilevel marketer won't help you, for example, if your business model involves selling direct to consumers over the Web.

4. Shift into *Engineer* mode once you have your business model down and the right people on board. The beauty of hiring great people who fit your business plan is that they can actually eliminate many of the issues you used to have with your systems and processes. But if they can't, then your job becomes clear.

5. Once the kink in the hose is resolved, put on the *Learner* hat again to find a way to accelerate growth for the business if things are going well. Perhaps it's a new target customer, a new product, or a new geography. Usually this also involves going deep into *Player* mode to understand the situation before handing the new initiative off to the organization to execute.

This should be a fluid and repeatable process, one that involves art and intuition and one that you, as the CEO, need to be constantly vigilant about. After all, the future of your business is at stake. In the chapters that follow, you'll learn more about each of the five hats you can wear to help solve the constraints you've identified and how you can take a more active role in eliminating them and supercharging your company's growth.

Now that we've covered the five hats in overview, it's time to go into depth on each of the hats and how they are used by highly effective CEOs once they have identified the point of constraint. If you know your point of constraint, jump right to the chapter that corresponds to it. If not, we are going to follow the hats in the order of their use.

KEY POINTS

- Constraints are controllable—if they are not in your control, they can't be constraints.
- Constraints lie in the following areas: economics (revenue, margin, assets); risk (negative impact to the business); pain (recurring difficulties, internally or with customers); or strategy (Mafia Offer, expansion opportunities).
- You might have a business model problem if there's a lack of momentum; there's a low gross margin, low profitability, low recurring revenue, or low return on capital employed; or a low-performing segment masks overall business performance.
- You might have talent problems if you cover for low-performing employees; you wouldn't rehire a particular employee; an employee is unwilling to learn or is not committed to team performance; or your people do not generate as many exciting ideas as you do.
- You might have process and system problems if you need to hire superstars all the time; your organization has trouble meeting its commitments; cycle time is poor; there are a lot of non-value-added processes (TIMWOOD); or your current systems and processes do not align with your target customers' values.
- Order of attack: List the potential points of constraint; rank them based on economic impact, risk, or pain; ties go to Architect; repeat. If all is going well, use the Learner hat to figure out what's next.

Chapter Two

THE LEARNER HAT

Never become so much of an expert that you stop gaining expertise. View life as a continuous learning experience.
—Denis Waitley

There is one hat that Lazy CEOs never take off: that of the Learner. One of the most pivotal roles any CEO can play within an organization is addressing the question, "What's next?" Since you've reached this point in the book, you now know that CEOs should be spending the bulk of their time working on solving the organization's point of constraint. If you are working on something with less than a twelve-month time scale, it is a tactic. Anything longer than twelve months is a strategy. Being a Learner means shifting into a longer time horizon, unless you are learning to find the point of constraint. When you have your short-term constraints under control—like solving an immediate need by hiring a new salesperson—it's important for you to spend time looking further out on the horizon, eighteen to twenty-four months out, to identify what the next big thing will be that drives the organization into the future. When you put your Learner hat on, it becomes your job to answer these key questions: What's possible? and What's next?

Denis Waitley emulated this behavior, reinventing himself from a naval officer to a fundraiser to a public speaker and a best-selling author across his career. This thirst for learning and sharing the learning with others was key to his success.

As CEO, you likely have skills and abilities that others in the organization might not have. That's especially true when it comes to your ability to look at the future of the organization from a unique vantage point. Your experience enables you to analyze events and connect dots over extended time frames—to identify dependencies and to perform an if-then analysis—like no one else could. You can take data and integrate them in a way others in the organization cannot. That's why the job of looking into the future is not something you can or should delegate. Strategy is a process best done by a limited number of people, with the CEO at the lead.

> When you put your Learner hat on, it becomes your job to answer these key questions: What's possible? and What's next?

MODEL LEARNING FOR YOUR ORGANIZATION

It's also critical for CEOs to model the behavior of being a Learner so they serve as a role model for the organization as a whole. It's like telling your kids to read when you haven't picked up a book in years. Every CEO's job is to model behavior they want embedded throughout the organization. They need to be thirsty for new knowledge and experiences that will open their employees' minds to new ideas.

Learning is a tool that can give your organization a competitive edge and help with better execution. Over the long term, companies and leaders who can learn quickly will triumph over organizations that learn more slowly. This attitude and behavior are particularly important in fast-growth, fast-change industries like healthcare or high tech, which can transform overnight or with a single competitor's product announcement. When everyone in an organization is striving to learn—whether it's how to become a better leader, how to deal with international organizations, or how to embrace new technology—you'll get better results.

Moreover, you'll find yourself ahead of the pack in understanding where future disruptions will come from if your organization can learn and adapt, and you'll know how you can position the organization to best take advantage of them as opportunities.

One CEO we know asked the normal questions after a project—"What went right?" and "What went wrong?"—but he added another interesting question, one born from his natural curiosity: "What was unexpected?" This key question led to many insights and improvements over the years. This simple idea embedded learning into his organization.

LIFELONG LEARNING

When people talk about learning, their first thought might be the notion of going to school or some other formalized version of how one might learn. But going to school for, say, an MBA or an advanced engineering degree is really only one of the options on the table. What's important to recognize is that learning is dynamic. We've come across CEOs who, even though they had not completed college or even high school, could still go toe-to-toe with any PhD or similar expert in writing papers or generating new ideas because of those CEOs' intense ability to learn outside the classroom. That's not a knock against formalized education, which is still a great way to improve skills, meet new people, and create new connections. It's more about having an attitude of embracing learning regardless of whether it's in a classroom or not. Learners understand that formal education is a beginning point. All they did was accelerate their learning process by going to school, but they never stop learning. The larger goal is for you and your organization to find ways to assess what's going on around you in the global market and then find ways to take advantage of those changing forces.

Key is to see everything as a learning opportunity, to be an avid Learner no matter what you're up to: international travel, a conference, a chance meeting with someone outside your industry, even a failed project. These are all opportunities to learn and expand your thinking. Wearing the Learner hat means you are always on the lookout for opportunities for mastery. While immersed, you should be asking "Why?" "Why not?" "What if?"

One of the leading indicators that a leader is *not* putting him- or herself in a position to learn is that the individual is doing too much teaching (e.g., delivering keynotes, participating in conferences, etc.). These folks get out of balance because their *outflow* of ideas is greater than their *inflow*. They find themselves transmitting more than they are receiving, which can be a real danger sign.

Another red flag is when we hear an executive say something along the lines of, "I'm too old to . . ." Whether it's learning a new piece of software or hardware, or even just a new way to look at the world around you, once you've turned off your ability to learn, you're sunk.

MAKE A SHIFT IN YOUR ATTITUDE

Another key concept to embrace is that you need humility to become a thirsty Learner. It's an area where many CEOs go wrong, since we all know you need to have a certain strength of ego and sense of self to do the job well, to believe you are right even when you don't have complete data. But a mistake CEOs make is when they start assuming they have all of the answers and there is nothing left for them to learn.

Strangely, this is a notion that boards of directors struggle with as well. Many boards believe that when they put a CEO in place, he or she should already know everything needed to excel in the job. That's why the board members went outside the organization to find a candidate as opposed to looking internally to fill the position. Now they can simply slap each other on the back, call it a day, and wait for the great results to roll in. This kind of attitude is especially prevalent among boards dominated by private equity firms. But if the CEO they've just hired says he or she needs access to resources in order to learn something new, well, you'll probably be able to hear a pin drop.

> Learning is *the* key that enables any business to grow.

Boards should be looking for a CEO who is curious. Someone who has a wide-eyed view of the universe. Someone who has an insatiable appetite for bringing new ideas into the organization so that it will keep learning and improving along with its leader. However, this is applied learning, not academic learning. The goal is to translate new knowledge into business impact. *Learning* is the key that enables any business to grow.

The best performers don't necessarily top the IQ charts as much as they excel at complexity of mental processing (CMP), a concept developed by organizational development expert Elliott Jaques. People with high CMP scores can integrate information in powerful ways and can look out over extended periods of time to understand the impact of certain events. When we're young, all we can think of is *now*, as in "I'm hungry, *now*," and "I want my toy, *now*." But as we get older, we begin to make more complex and long-term decisions, as in investing four years of our life to attend college. We do this knowing we are delaying our sense of gratification for a bigger payoff down the road in terms of acquiring skills, knowledge, and a job that we love.

People with high CMP scores also see how events are connected to each other in sequential, parallel, and dependent ways. For example, if you asked Henry Kissinger about how to achieve peace in the Middle East, he would likely begin his answer by citing the origins of religions two thousand years ago before diving into the current topics of oil rights, water, religion, politics, technology, energy, geography, and social trends, and then talking about the people who are going to be leading the charge in the region over the next fifty years. In other words, you're not going to get a one-word answer from men and women with high CMP scores because they don't see the world that way.

It should be the goal of every organization to have people with the highest CMP scores serving in senior roles and leading the charge. Why? Because this skill allows people to see into the future and know what is likely to happen or at least know where the inflection points are in the business. In order to compete in the fast-paced global economy, every organization needs people capable of integrating information in ways that create opportunities for growth and competitive advantage. Keanu Reeves breaking the code of the world around him in *The Matrix* is what we're talking about. Can you imagine what the future of your organization might look like if everyone had that power of insight?

LEARNING TECHNIQUES TO EMBRACE

The following are some tools and techniques that CEOs wearing the Learner hat can begin to embrace and model for everyone in their organizations.

GO INTO PLAYER MODE
Inc. CEO Project has found that Lazy CEOs spend 25 percent of their time in Player mode. (In chapter 6 we go into more detail

about wearing your Player hat.) The question is "Why?" The answer is to learn. ==There is nothing like immersion in something to develop insights and understanding you cannot achieve by reading a report.== This is particularly true when you are on the diagnostic journey to find the point of constraint.

When they are trying to learn about a particular point of constraint, perhaps in the customer acquisition process, great CEOs will dive into Player mode to dig deep and learn. While they are in Player mode, they ask questions about the business model, the talent, and the processes. Because they are lazy, the goal is to get out of Player mode as quickly as possible. They'll do this by developing deep understanding and then deploying talent and processes as they exit. The result of this time in Player mode is a permanent improvement in the business.

Early in my career, a division of my company that made critical automotive parts took a strike from their union labor force. The manufacturing employees walked out and picketed the firm. There were a few of these critical parts on every car, so the business needed to continue supplying them or risk shutting down the car production lines across America. The management team took over the production line and began to make the parts. Unfortunately, there were only sixty people in management to cover 130 union jobs. The team took this as an opportunity to improve processes, to streamline workflows, and to improve quality. With these improvements, they were ultimately able to cover production during the two-month strike. When the strike ended, only sixty laborers were called back, halving the labor cost per unit. The moral of this story is that deep immersion in a process is an opportunity to make improvements that never would have been seen from your cushy office.

JOIN A PEER GROUP

When Keith McFarland used the term "scaffolding" in his best seller *The Breakthrough Company* (Crown Business, 2008), he was referring to how the best CEOs have learned to reach out to peers outside their organization as a key way to build up their own abilities and reference points. One of the most powerful teachers any Learner could have is access to a CEO peer group. By joining such a group, you gain access to a network of individuals who can help you think and work through many of the most difficult issues your organization faces. You essentially create an advisory group that lends you their mental processing power to dissect your own issues. That is an incredibly valuable resource for any CEO, especially when it comes to those issues where there is no clear black-and-white solution. More important, the way to learn how to be a great CEO is to model other great CEOs, and a peer group will expose you to leaders of other great businesses and how they address their tough issues, accelerating your own CEO experiences.

It's important to distinguish a CEO peer group from a networking group. When it comes to finding the right peer group for you:

- Look for smaller groups, generally fewer than ten people, so every member will be able to get enough time on topic at each meeting to be useful.
- Look for groups that employ a professional facilitator, not a trained member of the group. This is a must to ensure that agreed-upon group processes are used, and that members are held accountable, as well as to compel members to achieve their highest potential.
- Look for a group made up of similarly sized firms from different industries that deal with approximately the same level of complexity in their businesses. As your company grows larger, this will be harder and harder to find.
- Look for a group that focuses on the point of constraint within the business, no matter how uncomfortable that

issue is. Since you are going to invest time and money in your peer group, it should be one of the most valuable things you do—and that means working at the point of constraint. If the program is good, the return to the development of the individual and the business should be vastly out of proportion to the input of time and money. The better programs in this area offer a guarantee and will refund the fees if there is not a material benefit within a designated period of time.

We know, of course, that most of the toughest issues that reach the desk of the CEO aren't easy to solve or even to assess in terms of how a decision will have residual financial or legal impacts down the road. There's often no one right answer for any of these problems; multiple options are likely to be available to you. Your peer group allows you to talk through those options and solicit feedback on which one might be best at the time.

Peer groups are so valuable in areas like this because, based on their own experience, CEOs can help you recognize the macro impact of your decision much more quickly than you could on your own. Just as important, you also have the opportunity to learn by working with your peers to solve their issues. It's like multiplying your learning opportunities tenfold, which is something so valuable you can't put a price tag on it.

LEARN FROM OTHER INDUSTRIES

One of the most counterintuitive ideas we can share when it comes to learning is that the real breakthrough answers for your business, the truly profound ideas, are going to come from outside your industry. This is true as well in deciding who makes up the peer group you join. It's hard for many executives to wrap their heads around these ideas. Stop and consider, though, what it might be like to attend a peer group made up of, say, a group of automobile dealers. Each of your peers runs a business almost identical to yours, and probably inherited it from their father just like you did. You've all run your businesses the same way they've always been run, and any changes have rippled through the industry. So where are the new ideas going to come from?

Some CEOs insist that they need to have other companies like theirs represented in their peer group because they think those CEOs are the only ones who could truly understand the problems and issues they are confronting. This kind of attitude is a mistake. The truth is that someone else has already solved just about every problem out there, but it was probably someone in another industry. What's so innovative about this kind of thinking is that if you can bring in new ideas from outside your sector, you can actually create a first-mover advantage for yourself over your competitors who continue to be stuck thinking like everyone else.

> One of the most counterintuitive ideas we can share when it comes to learning is that the real breakthrough answers for your business, the truly profound ideas, are going to come from outside your industry.

Consider the example of a company that helped people book transportation for international goods via ocean-bound shipping containers. Until recently, the shipping industry was fairly staid and conservative in how it operated: If you wanted to ship a container filled with your product, you simply had to visit each company's portal to see if they had extra capacity and to receive a quote and sign a paper contract if you decided to hire them. It was a very manual process.

This company looked at how companies operate in the hotel and airline industries, which are highly refined and automated and many years ahead of the ocean-bound freight market. The company ultimately created one portal where customers could research every shipping company and get quotes and book the freight in an instant. Because they were the first company to do this, they were the only one doing it! Yet, this was commonplace in the hotel and airline markets.

They also helped the shipping companies implement dynamic pricing, which gave customers discounts based on how early they booked their cargo and how full the ship was when they placed their order. Overall, this innovation was hugely beneficial to both shippers and their customers because it streamlined the entire process, making it more efficient and profitable for everyone involved.

The key takeaway here is that this company became a disruptor in its industry not because it came up with something new, but because it simply borrowed an idea from another industry.

MAKE TIME TO TRAVEL

Travel is one of those good things that you can certainly have too much of. But it's imperative that you, as a Learner, make time to travel—especially internationally. It can be either for business or for personal reasons since the goal is to get you out of your groove and into new environments that will stimulate your creativity. It's how you will begin to generate pages of new ideas to bring back into your business, ideas you might otherwise not have had the brain fuel to come up with.

MAKE READING A PRIORITY

People who read a lot are Learners by their very nature. And the interesting part is that you don't have to keep to a strict diet of business books to get in the habit of reading. In fact, you'll generate more ideas if you read broadly—spy thrillers, crime dramas, biographies, and other nonfiction—whatever tickles your fancy. We've come across many CEOs, for instance, who have been able to take good ideas that originated while they were reading a history book and apply them to the present day.

The point is to find material that will help you build up a habit of regular reading. Think about what kind of difference exists between a CEO who reads one book every other quarter, or two a year, compared to the CEO who reads one book each month. It doesn't seem like that big a difference, right? But jump ahead five years, and one CEO has read ten books while the other has read sixty. Who do you think is coming up with more ideas to bring back to the business?

PREPARING YOURSELF TO LEARN

Another key practice the most effective CEOs employ surrounds the notion that they *prepare* themselves to be ready to identify new ideas when they hear them. It's one thing to accept all of the data that you can absorb on a daily basis. But to truly process those data and turn them into information you can use in your business, you need to create some quiet time to reflect and give your brain a chance to keep up.

> It is nearly impossible for a human brain to shift from an immediate issue to an issue that is years in the future and then back again.

One of the ways you can do this is to create a state of flow by engaging in activities that will allow your brain to focus in the background on processing those data. These activities can be anything from running and playing or watching sports to gardening or taking a shower. The idea is to give your brain excess capacity to go to work and come up with ideas a few hours later that you likely would not have imagined without the intellectual break. It is nearly impossible for a human brain to shift from an immediate issue to an issue that is years in the future and then back again. We cannot answer an e-mail and then return to long-range planning readily.

Another example of how to prepare yourself to generate ideas is to find ways to make your sleep time—your dream state—as productive as possible. Your brain does some of its best work while you're asleep. The goal is to give it a lot of data to process before you drift off. To do that, you should spend a good deal of time thinking and reading about the key details on a thorny issue before heading to bed. Your brain will work while the rest of you is recharging. You'll be amazed eight hours later when you're in the shower and great ideas suddenly come in a flood.

MAKE INVESTING IN ORGANIZATIONAL LEARNING A PRIORITY
We've been discussing how you, the CEO, can best prepare yourself to become a Learner, but you should also be thinking about the different ways you can help develop other Learners throughout your organization. The best companies spend 1–2 percent of their annual revenue creating both formal and informal learning opportunities for their team members. You should be doing this for yourself as well. We've found that many CEOs find it difficult to spend that much on this mission, but it's critical that you do.

You might also want to consider modifying your organization's hiring habits in order to actively recruit and bring in Learners. In our experience, it is possible to interview and select for people who are good Learners. This would be a critical shift in thinking for you and your HR team, especially if you work in a fast-growth industry or company. If you focus on hiring someone just for their skills and experience, rather than focusing on someone who is capable of learning new skills over time, you could easily find that the growth of the business soon eclipses the first candidate's capability to keep up. While that first candidate can do what you may have hired him to do, the needs of your business will change along the way, and he may not be able to keep up. You might consider what programming languages you used during your education and what ones are in use today. If you hire programmers who aren't active Learners, they will be obsolete very quickly, just as your knowledge of an older programming language would be if you tried to help. That's why identifying Learners is so critical for the future success of the organization.

One way to find Learners is to look at prior behavior. Look for people who have changed industries along their career paths, and become experts in that new industry. Contrast this with someone who has worked within a single industry for twenty to thirty years. These folks, while clearly competent, might not bring enough innovative thinking because they have been running with the herd too long. Be careful not to hire people who, despite having deep and interesting experience, have had the same one year of experience repeated twenty times.

You can also look for folks who have high CMP scores—which is exactly the approach that Verizon and the U.S. military use—in order to find people who process information in complex ways and can ultimately lead larger organizations. For example, during the interview process you could ask candidates open-ended questions and see what kinds of answers you get. When you find someone giving you one-sentence black-and-white answers versus someone who sees the much broader picture—a candidate who, like Keanu Reeves' character, Neo, sees the Matrix for all its various nuances, connections, and dependencies—you will know who you want on your team.

You can also use these tests to find younger workers who have the potential to grow their CMP as they gain experience. Someone who might be a CMP 3 now, at age twenty-five, and has the potential to become a CMP 5 who can run a significant organization. It can be a huge advantage knowing which employees warrant bigger investments over time. That, of course, is also how you can continue to grow the organization—not just today and tomorrow, but well into the future.

BUILDING A BOARD

Your own learning is powerful, but building a mastermind group in the form of a board around you to help power your learning can multiply your results. One of the most common characteristics shared by entrepreneurs is a kind of innate self-confidence, an indomitable spirit that pushes you past the barriers that hold others back. The issue, of course, is that there might be a cliff on the other side of that barrier: something a set of good advisors could have alerted you to.

When their company reaches a certain size and level of maturity, many entrepreneurs begin to consider the notion of creating a board of advisors or a board of directors to help keep the company's growth on the fast track. The fear of making a mistake or missing a great opportunity underlies the need for a board as well as planning for succession and a day when the original entrepreneur will be less involved in the business. Certainly, some owners of privately held or family-run companies reject the notion of bringing in outsiders for fear they might lose control or disclose too much of their secret sauce, or because they believe that they don't need the advice or help from anyone else to achieve success.

But it's been our experience in working with thousands of successful, fast-growth companies that the companies that stand out—the ones that truly break through—rely on an advisory board or even a structured group of CEO peers to help chart their path forward. We have found that the act of making yourself, as CEO, accountable to someone else results in you making better decisions in the long run—including steering clear of obstacles and taking better and more productive paths to growth. It's not just the act of creating a board that matters, however. It's finding the right mix of advisors, where each individual member of the board brings a particular skill or fills a specific need. When added up, the wisdom of the crowd, a mastermind group, will exceed that of the individual. *We* are smarter than *me*.

Before we get into the details of how you should structure your board, it may be helpful to define terms. A board of advisors is a group of people assembled to offer advice on anything from business development and growth strategy to risk management and talent acquisition. Many companies dip their toes into the water by forming a board of advisors that eventually evolves into a board of directors. A board of directors is a group of individuals who also give advice but, in agreeing to serve on the board, have a legal and fiduciary responsibility to the shareholders of the company. To say that another way, the advice a CEO gets from an advisory board is nonbinding, whereas a board of directors can actually hire and fire the CEO. If you are considering going public or have a diverse set of shareholders, a board of directors is more appropriate.

> The companies that stand out—the ones that truly break through—rely on an advisory board or even a structured group of CEO peers to help chart their path forward.

The most important challenge is determining who should be on your board. To answer that question, we need to begin by defining the five different skill sets that a board member could bring to the table.

OVERSIGHT

Oversight is the classic governance role, in which a board member weighs in on key decisions such as the compensation packages for the CEO and other senior managers, monitors the company's compliance with regulations, reviews audited financials, and handles the management of any shareholder issues that may exist. This function makes sure the business follows the rules. Certainly, a privately held company could potentially have fewer of these issues to deal with than does one that has taken on investors. But the bigger point here is that the board can provide a level of objectivity when it comes to issues of risk management. In other words, board members won't be sipping the company Kool-Aid and can therefore be counted on to deliver solid, independent advice directed in the best interests of the company.

When you go about recruiting board members who will bring oversight skills with them, you should consider folks such as former CFOs, CPAs, partners in an accounting firm, and lawyers. To be clear, the idea in recruiting accountants and lawyers is not to get a discount on their services but to ensure that you get good objective governance and oversight advice for your company. It is actually better if the CPA or lawyer on your board doesn't do any work for the firm.

INSIGHT

When you look for insight, you're searching for individuals who can help you devise and improve the strategy for your company's growth. That means finding individuals who have an understanding of your industry and how you can grow your business. It's often best to find at least two board members who can perform this role in order to get a balanced view. Consider recruiting current or retired CEOs of other companies from your industry or even those who supply it. You could also consider recruiting CEOs from similar industries or a great strategist who is in a very different space. Senior business consultants can be useful in fulfilling this role as well. Again, the point is to find individuals who have been there and done that and who are willing to share their knowledge and experience of what to do—and what not to do—in growing your business.

MONEY

The money role comes down to recruiting board members who understand banking, finance, and mergers and acquisitions

(M&A)—especially if your company's growth strategy involves either making acquisitions or being acquired. This is particularly critical in capital-intensive businesses. In this case, you'll want to recruit individuals with experience in financial structures and liquidity events who can help properly finance your business and position it to get maximum value when it is time for a liquidity event. That means you'll want to recruit traditional bankers, investment bankers, M&A leads, or even an executive at an investment firm. If your company has taken on an investment from a private equity firm, they will already have a seat on your board and their representative can potentially serve well in the money role. It is worth noting that some private equity board representatives have a hard time balancing the needs of their fund and the needs of the business; the best do this seamlessly.

GOLDEN ROLODEX

Another critical role that board members can play is utilizing their social and business networks to make introductions and take your company to places you could never go on your own. Let's say, for example, that you're exploring different acquisitions. Ideally, your board member's name would appear in the Golden Rolodex within your industry and could put you in contact with the executives and investors of potential acquisition targets. Other examples include partnerships and talent acquisitions, where a good board member not only can make recommendations about who to pursue for, say, a VP of sales position, but also can jump-start the relationship by making a phone call that paves the way for a follow-up from the CEO.

Keep in mind that a board member needs to be willing to pick up the phone or make introductions on your behalf. It's not enough to just have industry connections; he or she needs to be willing to use the connections on behalf of your company's growth. Being listed in a Golden Rolodex is a particularly valuable asset for a board member to bring to any company that is doing business with the government. Someone with prior government experience—such as an admiral, general, or deputy chief of staff—knows the right people to connect with to reach the appropriate decision makers.

CEO SPARE

The fifth and final skill set you'll want to consider for your board is not a required one. In fact, it's conditional on whether you have any viable internal candidates in the organization who could step into the CEO role in the wake of some kind of catastrophic event. That means you'd like to have at least one board member who would be qualified to lead the company until the company could name a full-time successor. Even if you do have internal successors lined up, having a capable board member who could help smooth the transition—especially in a family-run company where successions can get personal—can make for an excellent risk-mitigating strategy.

Now that we know what roles should be represented on your board, it's time to evaluate how the folks you have tapped to be on it stack up.

BOARD SKILLS MATRIX

We have found that whether you are starting the journey of creating the board or you simply want to rethink the makeup of your current group of advisors, it is extremely helpful to create a simple matrix that highlights the five key areas and roles where your board can add the most value.

The idea is that you want to see a good balance of marks across the board, such as in Figure 2.1 following. If you find that you are heavy in some areas and weak in others, you might need to rethink the composition of your board. For example, there may be too many financial experts and not enough industry veterans to rely on. Using the grid can also help you identify particularly valuable board members who bring more than one skill to the table as well as those board members who don't seem capable of pulling their weight.

Board Member	Oversight	Insight	Money	Golden Rolodex	CEO Spare
Mr. Henry	X		X		
Ms. Mills		X		X	
Mr. Counihan				X	
Ms. Dyer	X	X			X
Mr. Greenberg			X		

Figure 2.1: Board skills matrix

Changes in board composition take time. Personal relationships, history, and prior good service should always be considered, but like any other talent position in the business, the wrong person can inhibit growth. It is the job of the CEO and the board chairperson to find a way to remove nonproductive board members who may have outlived their usefulness and to replace them with individuals who can be more helpful on the company's path forward.

At the end of the day, the value in creating a board is that the group's goal will be to protect the interests of the owners of the business and that, as an owner, you will get better direction if you give up some level of control and rely on their input, advice, and connections. Better yet, with your board's help, you'll be able to push the boundaries of your company's growth and creativity without having to worry about a fatal mistake.

CEO COACHING AND THE ROLE OF THE BOARD

A hearty round of congratulations usually goes around the boardroom for identifying and recruiting a successor for the retiring CEO of many years. Many directors believe that this critical decision puts in place a fully formed executive who does not require further development to reach his or her highest potential. This rarely is the case.

Development of senior executives, even those who have operated as a CEO of other firms, is a high-return activity due to the leverage generated on the operating and financial performance of the organization. The need to continue operating the business as well as the investment of time and money often get in the way of ongoing leadership development. In some cases, the CEO should be hiring the outside coaching organization, and at other times, the board should do the hiring to establish oversight of and feedback on the process.

THE NEED

Due to a lack of internal candidates, boards of directors generally look outside a company to obtain an individual who has more than enough experience and capacity to perform well as CEO at the organization's current size and level of complexity. The risk of bringing on a CEO from outside the organization, however, is that you won't know much about the individual. On the other hand, the choice to promote an insider also carries risk since that individual generally has not performed the function. The plus, though, is that you would have a far higher level of knowledge of the insider's makeup and prior performance. Bottom line? Either class of executive can benefit from development.

Top executive development is often a neglected area of organizational development due to the notion that one must be fully developed in order to perform in the senior-most function. This fallacy is held in companies that spend world-class amounts on developing and retaining their human capital broadly within the organization, as well as companies that grow rapidly and change their scope or business models, fundamentally changing the executive role every few years.

The good news is that the problem and the solution are relatively clear. A 10 percent improvement in CEO performance can generate material business and financial performance in the organization. A relatively small investment is required to obtain this improvement.

EXECUTIVE EDUCATION

Proper credentials are expected before someone takes the top executive office, particularly in larger firms, which invest early in potential future leaders to ensure that they have the needed knowledge in advance. Smaller firms are less fortunate.

When a board is faced with an executive who is missing certain functional knowledge, it is vital that these gaps get filled rapidly if they are critical to organizational success. A number of executive education programs can fill any knowledge deficiency. These include specific courses such as finance or product development. Education of this type is both moderately time-consuming and inexpensive, but it has only modest impact. Higher-level impact can be had with more comprehensive programs such as executive MBAs or extensive leadership courses. Such programs represent materially higher cost and time investment, but they result in higher levels of executive knowledge and impact.

ONE-ON-ONE COACHING

One-on-one coaching involves placing a seasoned leader alongside a newer executive to improve performance through specific situational observations and education. Ideally, the teachable moments are used to reinforce the changes desired to get better results. Every executive coach must be capable of having open and direct conversations about personal characteristics that impact their charge's effectiveness, strategic issues, management, talent, and organizational development. More data-based coaching involves personality testing, group dynamic analysis, discussions with subordinates, and using such survey tools as 360-degree reviews.

Executive coaching of this one-on-one class is generally engaged by a board looking to improve the performance of the executive with otherwise acceptable levels of results. Since the board hires the coach, they have the right and expect to receive feedback. This means nothing is fully confidential, although it is critical that the coach establishes trust and has the confidence of the executive that any issues identified will be dealt with professionally and appropriately.

The coach should be focused on making the client aware of gaps in behaviors and performance, educating him or her on desired behaviors and shifting behaviors and time allocations to those with higher business impact. The success of a coaching intervention should be measured through both business performance and improvement in the business and personal metrics from the original baseline. Clearly, the measurement of success needs to be out of the hands of the CEO and the coach to ensure they are unbiased.

Be aware that executive coaching is not a well-regulated space, and there are few certifications that ensure quality. Nor are there standard approaches to these types of engagements; each one is customized to the needs of the executive and the style of the coach.

Costs will be significant because coaches at this level tend to be very senior and they will be dedicating a lot of time to the client. Eventually the rate of learning will flatten and the impact of further involvement with that particular coach will lessen. This can happen in a few months, if a specific behavior is the target of the coaching, or in a few years for more comprehensive engagements.

STRATEGIC CONSULTATION

Strategic consultation is the classic professional service desired by the executive or a board when they are focusing on the business model. The advice can either be a broad look at the environment and the proper direction forward or an external evaluation of the planned strategy developed by internal teams.

While either of these can be useful to the organization, neither should be considered executive development. They are project-related investigations into particular topics. The board, the executive, and the leadership team will become more knowledgeable and data-based in their decision making on the topic at hand, but this generally will not carry forward to broader insights and improved executive performance.

As you've just seen on the preceding pages, there is a range of options for CEO development, and each has pluses and minuses, as summarized in Figure 2.2. Factors to keep in mind when you consider which to choose include: the impact on specific executive knowledge, the cost, how the option should be used, the impact on building a network, and the business network. An understanding of the CEO and his or her development opportunities should guide the decision.

We have previously discussed CEO peer groups and the profound impact they can have on CEO performance through focus on the point of constraint, accelerated learning, and modeling of other high-performing CEOs. Along with peer groups, we have included networking groups in this table, which are popular but have limited impact except to grow the contacts of the participant.

Development	Executive Knowledge	Cost	Use	Network Development	Business Impact
Executive Education	High	High	Short-term growth	Moderate	Moderate
Peer Groups	High	Moderate	Long-term growth	Moderate	High
Networking Group	Low	Low	Exposure	High	Moderate
One-on-One Coaching	Moderate	Moderate	Intervention	Low	Moderate
Strategic Consultation	Moderate	High	Intervention	Low	High

Figure 2.2: Analysis of CEO development approaches

We covered a number of ways that CEOs learn, from reading to traveling to going to school to diving deep into Player mode—and, to learn something new in order to make a breakthrough—spending time outside their core markets. Being a strong Learner may be the single most defining characteristic of a great CEO. If you have not yet mastered donning this hat, you are doomed to repeat the past and make limited progress toward building the firm you lead. Ultimately, you are going to work far harder than does the Lazy CEO who figures things out, makes improvements, and moves on.

KEY POINTS

- Model learning for your organization. If you don't, no one else will.
- Be a thirsty lifelong Learner.

- Embrace the following learning techniques: Player mode; CEO peer groups; finding breakthrough ideas; make time to travel; make reading a priority; using a board.
- Prepare yourself to learn by creating space and quiet in your life.
- Make investing in organizational learning a priority.
- Use a mastermind group in the form of a CEO peer group, advisory board, or fiduciary board.

Chapter Three
THE ARCHITECT HAT

A building has integrity, just as a man and just as seldom! It must be true to its own idea, have its own form, and serve its own purpose!
—Ayn Rand

There is a classic story about a man who came upon three masons working hard at their craft on the same project. He asked the first mason what he was doing. The mason replied, "I am doing my job, to earn money." The man then moved to the second mason and asked the same question. The second mason replied, "I am building a wall." When the man asked the third mason the same question, he thought for a second and then responded, "I am building a cathedral!"

Entrepreneurs are builders. They try to build great businesses, teams, and customer bases. But sometimes they don't think about the design of what they're building because it's just too tempting to jump in and start stacking bricks on top of each other. They tend to react to challenges and opportunities without thinking about the outcome. But there are enormous advantages to pausing that day-to-day, minute-to-minute mindset and thinking more like an architect would about the design of a house or a skyscraper or a cathedral. You need to be someone who thinks long-term about the design of the business, about who you are serving, and about how you are going to make money. The quotation from Ayn Rand's *The Fountainhead* that opened this chapter speaks to the strength of design and the internal integrity and purpose of a great building and a great business. Lazy CEOs face their business model like an architect would in designing any structure.

It can be very challenging for many entrepreneurs to take a fresh look at how their business is structured and to consider changing it once they have started. It's not uncommon to hear comments from entrepreneurs like, "I just don't know what to do to make this a better business." The key is to rethink your role when it comes to how you look at your business as a whole and the constraints holding it back from achieving your long-term vision for it.

In this chapter, you'll learn how to don your Architect hat to explore ways that you could either remodel or improve key components of your business to help ensure that it remains on the fast track of growth. There are ways to remodel your business that can yield impressive returns on that investment of time. Later on in the chapter we'll share five strategies for you to consider using to change up your company's current business model: Moat Building, Recurring Revenue, Capital Velocity, the Mafia Offer, and Simple Is Hard. But let's first take a look at what constitutes a great business model before we start discussing any remodeling that needs to be done.

GREAT BUSINESS MODELS

Great businesses seem to always have a few things in common. One of them is an elegant business model, something that serves as a great foundation for future growth. Consider a business like Demand Media, which creates websites that cater to avid hobbyists in a variety of vertical fields, like Trails.com, GolfLink.com, DailyPuppy.com, and GardenGuides.com. They create online communities that allow people with similar interests to connect, learn, and share information with each other. Unlike a more traditional media company that has an editorial staff to create content, Demand Media draws from each community of avid enthusiasts themselves, at no cost. For example, Trails.com serves as a hub for information about cool hikes around the world along with pictures, maps, and GPS coordinates to help you get there. You'll even find great tips like where to find water or the best place to set up your tent. Hikers excited to share information with other hikers provide all of this content—for free!

But from an Architect's view, the best part about Trails.com is that the site's users upload all that content at no cost to the business. While there might be a moderator or two and a few technologists to make sure everything is running smoothly, Trails.com has no need for a big staff of reporters or editors. They also generate revenue through Google ads, which are served up on the site so the company doesn't need to hire a sales staff charged with trying to land clients. This means the owners of the site simply serve up ads to their visitors and collect their money.

Plus, since Demand Media leases space on other companies' servers, their costs are extremely variable; they expand only when the business demands and when doing so does not require capital. In other words, they've constructed a great business model: low capital costs, high degree of recurring revenue, high margins, great barriers to entry (what we call a deep, wide strategic moat, which we will explain later in this chapter), and good capital velocity. This is why on the Internet you'll find plenty of copycat models of Demand Media's elegant design that cater to everything from fishing and needlepoint to photography and cute cats.

It shouldn't come as a surprise when companies like Demand Media, which have fewer employees and paying customers than a traditional media outlet does, garner massive valuations from investors. Why? Because it's more like the way we think about real estate development than a traditional business model. It's different. In this case, entrepreneurs like those at Demand Media look for pieces of property to invest in—a URL—and then develop it to the point where they could sell it for far more than they paid for the initial plot of cyberspace. Here's a simple comparison of how this better business model is valued: The iconic *Washington Post* was purchased for $250 million, while Demand Media recently had a market capitalization of $425 million.

Another company that has created an elegant model is LiquidNet, which established a marketplace for stock transactions off the floor of various stock exchanges. In the "black pool," investors can buy and sell large blocks of stock, which can be very difficult to do via more traditional capital markets. That's because once other investors and traders get word of someone selling a large block, they'll immediately work to drive down (or up, depending on the circumstances) the price of the transaction. With LiquidNet, institutional investors can acquire the stock they want—maybe a 100,000 shares of Apple or GM—without worrying about someone else manipulating the price.

LiquidNet's computers are plugged into their members' order books. LiquidNet then automatically matches up those buy and sell orders. Customers are willing to pay a few pennies per share for that kind of confidentiality, speed, and anonymity. It adds up to several hundred million dollars in annual revenues for the company. Because the business is highly automated, with a small team of employees to acquire and work with the members and others who make sure the computers remain in top shape, LiquidNet's EBITDA is exceptional as a percentage of revenue. Further, the more members the company signs up, the more valuable the network becomes for everyone. Low capital costs, sticky and recurring revenue, high margins, a network effect: LiquidNet is a great business. The best part? It is replicable in other exchanges around the world and other asset classes—in a word, there is a clear pathway to growth.

When it comes to rethinking your business, sometimes you're best served by understanding the true drivers of revenue and profit. Sometimes it's not the material movement but the data movement that provides the real value. Consider a grocery store. The most important metric in terms of tracking a grocery store's performance is profit per square foot of floor space. The higher the revenue, the more profitable the store can become. So how would such a store go about maximizing its revenue in this way? The answer is probably in your wallet or on your key chain.

Like most people, when you go to your neighborhood store, you probably take out a plastic card the store gave you that offers you great discounts on certain products. Whether you realize it or not, that little card is the real key to the entire grocery business. The ability to track customer behavior lets the store know details such as forty-year-old women with kids tend to buy four gallons of milk every week, and, more specifically, when such a mom comes in and buys two gallons of milk, she also purchases a package of high-margin cookies most of the time. This information is incredibly powerful for helping shape the business. If a grocery store is good at analyzing the data it gathers from every purchase, it gives them an advantage when it comes to stocking up on inventory and running promotions that will help drive up that revenue and profit-per-square-foot metric. In that way, the store might be willing to give you customized offers to get you to the store in order to track your behavior because you are helping them establish a pattern that will make them far more money over the long run.

> When it comes to rethinking your business, sometimes . . . it's not the material movement but the data movement that provides the real value.

> **Attributes of Great Business Models**
> - Lots of recurring revenue (generally over 50 percent)
> - High gross margins (over 50 percent)
> - Low capital requirements (under $0.10/$1.00 of revenue)
> - Great return on assets employed (close to 100 percent)

REMODELING YOUR BUSINESS

A widely acclaimed chef once said that the key to a great steak dinner is starting with a great steak. Similarly, great businesses begin with a great business model. So the key question you need to ask is, how strong is my company's business model? Depending on your answer, perhaps you need to ask this follow-on question: Is it time for us to dig in to find the cracks in the company's foundation before it's too late to remodel? These ideas about business models can be used when creating a new model or working to improve an existing business. Here are a few strategies to consider: Moat Building, Recurring Revenue, Capital Velocity, Mafia Offers, and Simple Is Hard.

STRATEGY ONE: MOAT BUILDING

You probably recall from a high school history class or perhaps from watching *Game of Thrones* that a moat is essentially a barrier that protects a castle from any pesky invaders who may want to climb its walls. You want wide moats around your business to protect it from the invading forces of competitors.

When Warren Buffett, the so-called Oracle of Omaha, speaks, people listen. That's because he's been a fabulously successful investor, someone who has learned how to assess risk and who knows what makes a business a good bet. His advice to the leaders of his various businesses is that a year spent making the business more defensible and revenue assured—expanding your moat—is more important than making the revenue or profit in a given year. Why? Because the more work you do to make it harder for your competitors to take your customers, the more you ensure your own survival and profitability. Buffett's simple maxim when selecting businesses is "*Economic castles protected by unbreachable moats.*"

When it comes to your business, you need to be thinking about strategies akin to building an alligator-filled river of sludge around your castle, making it difficult and painful for any of your competitors to cross over into your market. Obtaining patents is one great example of something you can use to make it harder for your competitors to get into the same business you're in.

When your organization is trying to open up markets, having to spend two years testing, writing specifications, and attending meetings, don't view it as a slog. Instead, try thinking of that process this way: As hard as it is for you, it would be just as hard, if not harder, for the next firm that tries to follow. This is especially true if you create some kind of moat around the business. Great firms—and their great CEOs—commonly protect themselves with these popular moats: data moats, network moats, intellectual property moats, switching-cost moats, speed moats, and talent moats.

> **Data moat.** The credit bureau industry creates value by aggregating data from all of the different things you've done with your money, from taking out a Macy's or an American Express charge card to paying off your mortgage and car loans. They employ a business model that paints a complete financial risk profile of each of us. It would be extremely hard for a new entrant to penetrate this market because of the comprehensive nature of the data and the thousands of data sources they would need to paint a similarly complete picture of a borrower. Strategically, they are constantly looking for additional data

streams they can use to create an even more accurate picture, increasing the size of their data moat.

Network moat. The impact of the network effect can be a strong element of an excellent business model. The more people who use the service, the more valuable it becomes to everyone involved. Once a network-based business gets critical mass, it is extremely difficult for new entrants to catch up. It becomes a very sustainable revenue generator. Robert Metcalfe, co-inventor of Ethernet and founder of 3Com, coined Metcalfe's Law regarding telecommunication, social, and other networks, but it is appropriate for any network-based business. Metcalfe's Law states that the value of a telecommunications network is proportional to the square of the number of connected users of the system.

Intellectual property moat. A strong trade secret and patent portfolio can be a powerful element of a durable business model. Consider QUALCOMM, with its extensive patent portfolio on mobile communications chips. Their position is so strong that it would be hard to name the second-best firm in the space. Of course, in the pharmaceutical industry, intellectual property is the name of the game and drives the ability to make money with big drugs.

Switching-cost moat. Increasing the cost and pain that a customer has to endure to switch from your brand to a competitor's is an age-old way to make your business last. Because customers have become very savvy to this approach, you will need to provide value in order for them to give up the future option to switch. An excellent example of this value is a free cell phone like the ones cell network operators offer in exchange for a two-year contract. Note that a data-transfer moat, which we discuss later, is a specific example of a switching-cost moat.

Speed moat. The speed with which your processes operate is a sustainable advantage. The adage "The large don't eat the small; the quick eat the slow" is true. This can be the case whether you are a quick product innovator, able to speedily deliver products, or you are able to acquire customers faster than your competition does. Each of these is a powerful advantage if leveraged commercially and can drive growth and profits to market-leading figures.

Talent moat. You can also build moats around talent, especially in technical fields where you essentially hire all of the world-class A players, leaving only the Bs and Cs for your competitors to lean on. (This is something we'll discuss in more detail in chapter four in the context of wearing your Coach hat.)

Lazy CEOs follow Buffett's advice and spend a lot of their time on expanding the size of their moats, which in turn improves the predictability and longevity of their businesses. In fact, they are very willing to sacrifice short-term financial performance to improve the business model.

STRATEGY TWO: RECURRING REVENUE

There's an inconvenient truth in business that most CEOs and entrepreneurs tend to overlook: Not all revenue is created equal. Sure, a dollar in sales is a dollar in sales. But the more predictable that dollar is—as in it being likely that you will receive that dollar from your customer every month—the more valuable it becomes. When you begin to multiply that dollar by adding new customers and creating an annuity of cash flow, you begin reaping the benefits of what is known as a recurring revenue stream.

The concept is closely related to the notion of the lifetime value of a customer. If you were a car dealer, for example, you might be able to sell a car to a customer for $25,000. But that's a single transaction; you might not see that customer again for another seven or so years. However, if you could get that customer to also service and maintain his or her car through your business—and maybe even finance it as well—you would have created a recurring revenue stream from that one customer over the long term. These secondary streams can be even more profitable than the original transaction is. The companies that understand this equation are even willing to make little or no money on a customer in year one or two because keeping that person for the long term and making more money later is much more powerful.

An example of this is ADT Corporation, which provides security systems. ADT actually uses a direct sales force and a dealer network to market and acquire customers. When you sign up with ADT, you sign a three-year monitoring contract. ADT knows that once you clear the three-year mark, you are likely to continue—perhaps for another five to seven years! To get you to that point, ADT is willing to pay its dealers a significant portion of the revenue from that three-year contract because they understand the value of attracting you as a customer for the next decade or more.

Recurring Revenue Is a Powerful Growth Strategy

Lazy CEOs love recurring revenue. What makes recurring revenue so valuable is that you can spend more of your energy growing your business rather than on trying to acquire enough new or repeat business just to hit the same revenue level you did the year before. Let's say you run a business with $10 million in sales, 90 percent of which is recurring. Since you can already bank on receiving $9 million as you kick off your next fiscal year, you need to find just an additional $1 million to match your prior year's result. Anything you add beyond that is all growth. Compare this to a business built with no recurring revenue. You might sell $10 million one year, but every subsequent year you begin again at $0, making it tough to sustain growth. Which business would you rather run? And, just as important, which one would appeal more to a buyer or an investor?

With recurring revenue you can predict most of what you're going to earn and you face less risk, something that investors love. (One private equity firm even hands out bumper stickers that say, "I ♥ recurring revenue.") In fact, the more recurring revenue a company has, the higher the valuation it will receive from prospective buyers and investors. That's why recurring revenue has become the gold standard of business models and something that every CEO should be working toward building into their own businesses.

You need only compare the fate of Blockbuster with that of Netflix to see the power of this idea. While both firms rented DVD-based movies to consumers, Netflix has essentially 100 percent recurring revenue and Blockbuster had almost none. What was left of Blockbuster just before its bankruptcy was a market capitalization of under $20 million, while at the end of 2015, the market valued Netflix at more than $49 billion. The market is valuing every dollar of Netflix trailing revenue at over $7 to arrive at that market capitalization. That's compelling evidence of the power of recurring revenue.

Once again, ADT serves as an excellent example of this power. At the close of 2015 it had a market capitalization of $5.35 billion with revenues of $3.57 billion. The market at the end of 2015 valued every dollar of revenue at ADT at $1.50. In contrast, we can look at Ford Motor Co., which has revenues of some $147 billion, yet its market cap is $55 billion, which means the market values every dollar of revenue it generates at just $0.37. Why the difference? Because ADT has low capital needs and recurring revenue with lifetime customers, and Ford is still stuck with a largely transactional, capital-intensive business. We repeat: Not all revenue is created equal.

Add Recurring Revenue Streams to Existing Products

Consider the example of Philips, which conducted a company-wide drive many years ago to add service offers on all of their product-based businesses, even medical imaging systems. Sales had been growing due to global demand, but once a customer in, say, Indianapolis bought a new MRI for the local hospital, they might not need another one for quite a while. This is a classic example of a nonrecurring revenue stream. By adding service consulting, contracts, spare parts supply, training, overhaul service, and financing services around the sale of the imaging equipment, Philips created several recurring revenue streams that were far more profitable and valuable than was the sale of the equipment. In other words, every dollar of product revenue also generated a few trailing dollars of revenue from services and, over time, the money and margins made from services exceeded that brought in from product sales.

There are actually five kinds of recurring revenue: Repeat; Basic Recurring; Contracted Recurring; Sequential and Recurring; and Networked Recurring. These can be arranged in a value pyramid in which the higher your business model sits within the pyramid, the more valuable it is. And the key to value in this case is the ability of your business to create barriers to entry for competitors while also making it undesirable for your customers to switch their business. Think of these barriers as moats. The deeper and wider your moat, the more effective it is at repelling competitors. Let's expand on each of these five kinds of recurring revenue.

Repeat Revenue Level One of the pyramid is called Repeat Revenue, based on repeat customers. Let's say your business is a local grocery store. Having neighborhood folks stop by every few days to pick up staples like milk and eggs is a great thing. By providing solid customer service, you can hope to attract those same customers on a weekly basis for years. The problem is that there is really nothing stopping your customers from shopping at a new store that opens closer to their homes. Other than the possible higher cost of fuel and inconvenience, the customer incurs no switching costs. The strategic moat around this business is narrow and shallow. While having repeat customers is better than not having them, your revenue stream remains risky because you can't count on your customers sticking with you. Many firms in this mode have built affinity programs, like frequent flyer cards, to create stronger brand preference and to make their offers stickier, thus increasing the size of their moat.

Basic Recurring Revenue Level Two of the pyramid is called Basic Recurring Revenue, where you find businesses such as insurance agencies and cable companies that benefit from a basic level of recurring revenue. Think about when you sign up for your auto insurance policy. You agree to pay a certain amount of money every month for a year, which makes for a fine source of recurring revenue. But, as with the grocery store, your customers are under no contractual obligation to renew their policy with you or even to stick with you for the life of that policy. Customers can simply shop around and, if they find a cheaper rate, instantly switch over their policy, robbing you of what you thought was bankable income. Some businesses have worked to combat this by adding automatic credit card or bank account billing, which can be effective in changing the consumer's decision either to stop or to continue the service each month. By doing so, you create a negative option or opt-out model, which makes it easy to continue and difficult for the customer to stop paying for a service. That in turn drives up retention rates.

Contracted Recurring Revenue Level Three of the pyramid is called Contracted Recurring Revenue. Think about the contract you signed when you got your new cell phone. Not only did you agree to pay a certain amount of money each month depending on the plan you selected; you also agreed to keep paying for a specific period of time. Sure, you can change your phone provider, but it will cost you. You may have to pay a $200 or higher switching fee. That's a moat that'll make you think twice before you jump, which makes for a better business model. The phone company also runs promotions offering a discounted new phone every year or so. Of course, there's a catch: You need to sign a new two-year contract to take advantage of the offer. The exchange of a highly discounted phone for a two-year revenue contract is a good deal for the carrier. Again, this is an appealing model because the carrier can predict with a higher level of certainty what its recurring revenues will be both in the short term as well as over the longer term.

A related example is the business model employed by Salesforce.com, the online customer relationship management (CRM) provider. Customers of Salesforce.com don't have to sign a long-term contract; they pay a fee per user, per month. At first you might think this is simply an example from Level Two of the pyramid. After all, what's to stop customers from switching to a competing website? Well, in this case, there is actually a convenience cost to switching. Consider that the more you use Salesforce.com to track your contacts and appointments, the more data you accumulate. And since those data are stored on a database hosted by Salesforce.com, you will have to jump through some technical hoops to transfer them to a competing service, making it far more likely that you'll just stay put. Of course, the company will promise that changing is possible—even easy—but in fact it is quite difficult.

The harder you can make it for your customer to switch, the less risk there is to your recurring revenue and the future of your business. We call this a data transfer moat where it becomes easier for a customer to keep using a service than to switch to another one. This isn't some nefarious practice; customers can change if they want to.

It's more of a strategy to make them ask themselves why they would even want to go through the trouble of switching.

Sequential and Recurring Revenue   Level Four of the pyramid is called Sequential and Recurring Revenue. The idea behind this approach is to create recurring income by encouraging your customers to consistently upgrade to new product and service offerings. Look no further than multibillion-dollar companies like Microsoft and Oracle to see how this model works. Take, for example, Microsoft's flagship software product, Microsoft Office. Initially you might purchase Office 2010. A few years later, Office 2013 comes out with several fancy new features to tempt you to upgrade to the new product. Microsoft has recently shifted its model to more recurring revenue with a subscription-based model, Office 360. If that's not enough to convince you, consider that the company may also issue an alert saying it will stop supporting earlier versions of the software. Either way, Microsoft has found a way to keep collecting money from you. These upgrades are planned, and they are a primary way to drive revenue for the business.

Oracle takes a more component-driven approach in which it encourages its customers to constantly upgrade by adding new features. The company might begin, for instance, by selling you an enterprise resource planning (ERP) system. Of course, there is a maintenance and upgrade stream on this base product. Then, in time, Oracle will try to entice you to add such complementary components to your system as a customer relationship management (CRM) or a human resource management (HRM) system, each time adding new levels of service and charges. This concept was the driver behind Oracle's acquisitions of JDE, Siebel, and PeopleSoft over the years.

Or take a company like Constant Contact, which starts customers out on a basic plan that costs $10 per month. As you begin to use the system more, you can then upgrade if you like, spending an additional $5 per month to get unlimited image storage or the ability to input a larger number of contacts. In other words, the more you use the system and the more valuable it becomes to you, the more you're willing to pay, which results in the creation of a significant data moat. This model also works when companies offer a free service as a way to attract new customers. Think about DropBox, which provides a certain amount of free storage, or LinkedIn, which is free to use but offers premium access as well, enabling customers to access advanced features. Even if a company like DropBox or LinkedIn can convert just a fraction of its customers over to the premium service, it can create an extremely valuable sequential, and thus recurring, revenue stream.

Networked Recurring Revenue Level Five, the highest level of the pyramid, is called Networked Recurring Revenue. The more someone uses the company's product or service, the more each individual customer gets out of the experience—what we call the network effect (referred to earlier as one of the moats you can build around your business)—which creates a barrier to that customer leaving. Consider the appeal of a company like eBay. Regardless of whether the user is a buyer or a seller, the more people who participate in the company's online auctions, the more valuable it becomes for those buyers and sellers—to the point that they wouldn't even consider switching to a competing offering. Can you even name a viable competitor to eBay these days?

An example of a more recent start-up that uses this model is Groupon, which offers a deal of the day to the members of its social network. The model is premised on the notion that deals, such as a discount to a restaurant or tickets to a show, become viable only if a certain number of people sign up for them. Online dating services such as eHarmony have a similar model; the more people who participate, the more potential soul mates are available and therefore the higher probability that you will find yours. LiquidNet and LinkedIn work similarly. Customers and advertisers are less likely to leave these services since they risk losing the benefits of remaining in the community. The secret to these businesses is getting to critical mass before any other firm does and then becoming the de facto standard.

Whether you're the CEO of a company or an entrepreneur hammering out your first business plan, you need to be thinking about how you can drive a higher percentage of the five kinds of recurring revenue through your company. Even if you can move from 0 to 15 percent recurring revenue, you will

> Whether you're the CEO of a company or an entrepreneur hammering out your first business plan, you need to be thinking about how you can drive a higher percentage of the five kinds of recurring revenue through your company.

have done wonders for the value of your company. Ideally, we'd never see another business started that didn't have recurring revenue woven in. The point is that if you're not thinking along these lines, you're putting the future of your business in jeopardy.

How to Add Recurring Revenue to Your Business

When Jack Welch took over at GE back in 1981, he was handed the reins to one of the most innovative and diversified companies of all time. Founded more than a century ago, GE expanded by selling a range of big-money products such as medical imaging machines, locomotives, and jet engines. What's interesting, though, is that once GE sold a jet engine to, for instance, an aircraft manufacturer, the relationship essentially ended until it needed another. This troubled Welch. He recognized that relying on a one-and-done business model was crippling the growth engine of the company.

As a Lazy CEO, Welch helped shift the mindset of GE from a company that sold products to a company that sold only bundles of products and services and established a long-term relationship with their customers. Thereafter, when GE sold a jet engine, it also sold lucrative and recurring service contracts, spare parts supply, and overhaul and financing services along with it. GE could afford to sell the engine at cost, knowing that it would earn its margin from the support services instead. The profit was no longer in the product! Now, rather than watch its customers walk away after closing a deal, GE could count on receiving a steady and profitable revenue stream for as long as that engine was in service. This business model shift powered the company's growth and profitability for a decade.

So what does this story have to do with your company? Sure, you recognize that recurring revenue trumps nonrecurring revenue in every hand, since businesses with recurring revenue are more profitable, are easier to run, are easier to grow, and provide a better and more stable work environment to their employees. But that's not the business model on which your business was founded. "If I had it to do all over again, I would have done it differently," you might say. "But now it's too late." The story of one-hundred-year-old GE proves that it's never too late to make the switch. While your company might not have GE's deep resources, there are several options you can consider to make a significant shift in your business on the fly.

Another example you might not be as familiar with is a client of ours that provides IT services for government agencies, Merlin International, whose CEO is David Phelps. Even though the company had already passed $150 million in revenues, only 20 percent was recurring from some maintenance contracts. Over a five-year period, they made a concerted effort to shift their focus from selling hardware and software to selling longer-term service contracts. At the end of those five years, the company still reported $150 million in revenue, but $110 million of that was recurring revenue, which completely shifted the value, stability, and long-term potential of the business.

If you want to emulate that kind of switch in your business, the first step is to stop digging the hole any deeper. It's amazing how many business owners settle for the status quo even when the future of their business is at stake. Just because you've always sold your products a certain way doesn't mean you should continue doing so into the future. To be clear, it's a great thing that you successfully sold your products in a nonrecurring way in the past. You know better than anyone: It's really hard work. But as you begin to introduce upgraded product versions 2.0 and 3.0, it's a perfect opportunity to do so in a way that takes advantage of recurring revenue.

Let's look at a number of options for how you can begin adding recurring revenue components to your product company today.

Service One straightforward way to add a recurring revenue component is to start servicing your products post-sale. The mistake many entrepreneurs make is treating service as purely a customer support function, doing it free or below cost as opposed to treating it like a profit center. Offering service is not simply a way to take money from your customers. They need service and you, as the maker of that product, are uniquely qualified to service it. By offering service, you have a license to charge fees for that service, similar to any other firm. Consider the example of an auto dealership. These businesses typically don't make a lot of money selling cars. Their bigger profit comes from performing brake jobs, oil changes, and other major and minor services to the cars they sell. By coming up with recommended maintenance schedules, the dealers also found a way to remind and encourage customers to come in for service on a regular basis. Let your customers know that your product requires regular servicing to perform optimally and that your company is best suited to provide it.

The same goes for insurance or warranty policies. Best Buy uses these to remarkable success to help counter the fact that margins in the electronics business are so tight. While electronics stores have some of the highest revenue-per-square-foot marks around, their margins per square foot are near the bottom. That makes Best Buy's success curious. Invariably, when you go into a Best Buy store to buy an expensive gadget, they will offer to sell you a warranty on it to protect your investment. And apparently many people purchase those options because more than 50 percent of the company's profits result from those warranty sales. (In some years it represented 100 percent of their profits!)

Not only can you offer to service your own products, you should also be expanding into servicing and maintaining your competitors' products as well. Doing so builds intimacy with your customer and gets you "inside the tent." When your customer begins to think about buying a replacement product, you have already positioned your company at the front of the line to provide guidance and compelling alternatives. You might even be able to recommend when they should replace an older competitive product. There is the additional advantage of learning where your product might be ahead or behind in its feature set. If you learn that you have fallen behind, you can begin to catch up by learning the ins and outs of your competitors' products and incorporating those insights into your own product's design cycle.

Maintenance Contracts   At first glance, selling copy machines might not seem like the snazziest business model around. But when you look closer, there is actually a very compelling lesson to be found in recurring revenue. Such businesses have extended and enhanced the service models offered by car dealers through their innovative use of all-inclusive ownership contracts that include maintenance. Rather than simply sell products, such businesses lease their copiers and add fees that cover the ongoing maintenance of the product. If a customer insists on buying the copier, on the other hand, they will find that the cost of a typical service call outside of a maintenance contract makes for a poor economic choice. Not only are maintenance contracts a great way to build recurring revenue for your business, they also guarantee that their product will be calibrated every six months and will be repaired or replaced if it breaks, all of which is covered in a single monthly payment and greatly helps to ensure a customer's satisfaction.

Training Another recurring revenue stream to consider is offering training fees for your product. This can be particularly useful to your customers if you make a product that is sophisticated or complicated to operate. This is a win for both parties since your customers will get more value out of the product if they fully understand how to use it, and the offer will be stickier if they are getting full value. Again, you can also offer training services built around your competitors' products as a way to gain competitive intelligence and strengthen your customer relationship.

Financing Building a recurring revenue stream out of financing can take several forms. For instance, you could offer your product on a lease-to-buy basis, where the customer pays you a monthly fee for three years until they take ownership. You can earn a margin on such a deal, especially if you can secure favorable terms from your lender. Let's say you can borrow money at 5 percent and then charge your customer 9 percent. You have then earned a 4 percent spread on the deal. This extra profit comes with minimal effort. You will likely increase your total sales as well if you can provide reliable financing for your product.

Some firms do not sell products, as in our copier example. They make their product available only through a monthly rental fee.

The beauty of this approach is that there is no end to the payment stream. While paying down the financing, you will make the spread in the cost of money and the price of money. Once the loan is paid, the entire payment is profit to you. This is a particularly powerful approach if you have a balance sheet that can accommodate the lending. If you don't have a strong balance sheet of your own but have a strong financial partner willing to help, you can still provide this. In other words, financing can be a very profitable source of recurring revenue and is often overlooked by entrepreneurs.

Bundling   Up to this point, we've discussed single line item approaches to adding recurring revenue to your business. The most effective and profitable approach, though, can often be bundling up maintenance, training, and financing into an array of services, which you provide your customers for a recurring fee. Instead of selling your product for $50,000 the way you used to, you can now charge $2,500 a month for the guarantee that you will maintain the product, you will train your customers' people on how to use it, and you will fix it if it breaks. The copier business has translated this to a per-copy charge with all of the services bundled into this single charge.

By bundling you have also combined the fees you earn on financing in a way that prevents your customers from going outside your relationship and attempting to borrow money on their own. You have also instantly created multiple recurring revenue streams from a single product and realized all of the income from multiple sources. And you have "bear-hugged" your customers and made it hard for others to displace you.

Making the Shift

At this point you might be saying, "I love the idea of shifting to a recurring revenue business model, but I'm not sure my customers will go for it." Making the shift from nonrecurring to recurring revenue along the lines that we've discussed will indeed require effort to educate your customers about the benefits of the change. Your basic approach, therefore, should focus on showing how, by handling maintenance of your product during its lifetime, you allow your customers to focus on doing what they do best. If you make the machine that produces their product, they can focus on selling those products rather than hiring their own employees to maintain it.

You can also demonstrate to your customers that your new service bundle will benefit their cash flow. Since they no longer have to allocate a big chunk of capital to purchase the product, they can match their cash outflow with the cash coming in from their customers. This minimizes their exposure to changes in technology as well. Some firms will offer a service bundle that ties directly to the use of the machinery. Costs for support and maintenance track the use of the equipment.

Unfortunately, no matter how much effort you put into educating them, you will likely receive pushback from at least a few of your customers. If you face this hurdle, you can consider such options as splitting your customer base into two groups: one in which the people pay the recurring fee, and the other in which the people are charged according to your older, traditional nonrecurring model. You can then make it clear that you intend to terminate your support of your older products after a certain period of time and that service calls are going to be expensive. Granted, this approach takes some guts, since it will require you to redouble your efforts at educating those customers who are resisting the shift. But, if you stick to your guns, you'll find that as more and more customers migrate over to your new offering, you've found a strategy to upgrade your business and your customer base over time.

Making the shift to add recurring revenue streams will also transform your business, especially when it comes to designing future generations of your products. In the past, your engineers might have been willing to take shortcuts in their designs or material choices because they knew a customer would be responsible for paying for repairs and defects. But if your company is now responsible for supporting your products, you'll need to retrain your engineers to find ways to ensure that your support teams aren't unduly tied up. By taking control of the service of your products, you have brought your engineers into better alignment with your customers as well as with your revenue model. The concept of total cost of ownership will have real power, since your company will be fully exposed to the lifetime cost of operation.

In the end, building recurring revenue capabilities into your products is a good deal for both you and your customer. You will create better products, have a more reliable revenue stream, and foster a tighter customer relationship. Your users will be able to focus more on their businesses and have cash outflow that more closely matches their cash inflow. To get there, though, requires a significant mental shift by both parties. This ability to make strategic shifts, however, is what separates Lazy CEOs like Jack Welch and David Phelps and companies like GE and Merlin International from all the rest. When it comes to your business, there is no time like the present to take the first step in that new direction.

STRATEGY THREE: CAPITAL VELOCITY

An entrepreneur recently started a new business and asked me for advice on the most important things to remember in running his company. My answer? Rule #1: Don't Run Out of Cash! Rule #2: Don't Run Out of Cash! And Rule #3: Don't Run Out of Cash! Businesses go out of business due to a lack of cash, *not* because they aren't profitable.

The smartest entrepreneurs understand the power of cash in their business and how even a profitable operation can fail without it.

That's why one of the key concepts every CEO can focus on is the velocity of their money, which, simply put, is how quickly you turn your company's cash over each year. And at Inc. CEO Project we've found that the most successful CEOs spend a significant amount of their time making sure their money velocity rate is as high as it can possibly be.

> We've found that the most successful CEOs spend a significant amount of their time making sure their money velocity rate is as high as it can possibly be.

Let's create a simple example where you count up the amount of inventory you have on hand and then add your accounts receivable—the amount people owe you—and then subtract whatever you owe other people—accounts payable. This leaves you with your net working capital.

To calculate your capital velocity, which is how many times your capital is used to make your full margin, divide your annual gross margin by your net working capital:

Capital velocity = (Annual Gross Margin $/Working Capital $) x 100 percent

In a lower-margin business with higher capital velocity, you might see a capital velocity of 100 percent, meaning you created a margin equal to the working capital. It is not uncommon to see capital velocity over 500 percent in well-run companies.

The higher the capital velocity rate the better, because it means your business is generating more cash on a regular basis. If you turn your cash rapidly—low inventory and receivables of fifty-two times with customers who pay quickly—it means you turn your margin fifty-two times a year, or, in other words, you need only seven days' worth of cash to run the business. If you turn just four times a year, you need ninety days' worth of cash, which might put your business at risk of running out of money. If your annual net margin is $20 million and you have $10 million of cash in the business, you have a capital velocity of two turns. Increases in margin and decreases in working capital are both ways of increasing capital velocity.

A great example here is McDonald's. It purchases its hamburgers from a supplier that gives the company thirty-day terms, and there's very little inventory, just a few days' worth, in each restaurant. Customers pay for the product in cash and consume it before McDonald's needs to pay its supplier! It has negative working capital on the burgers.

Walmart has a similar arrangement with Procter & Gamble. P&G puts products into Walmart on consignment, and Walmart pays fifteen days after it sells the product. Zero inventory, no accounts receivable, and fifteen-day terms with suppliers: There are no cash limits to growth with this model.

One of the roles of the Architect in this case is to question how the business can improve its capital velocity. Strategies here could include the following:

> **Use customers to fund your business.** Thinking about improving money velocity could be an opportunity for the business to consider ways to change its business model to incorporate something like a membership model, where customers pay in advance or even place a partial advance payment for their services or products. We worked with one start-up company, for instance, that was involved in developing a software product that collected advance payments from five clients and used that capital to finalize the product, thus avoiding any need to go to the market to get additional capital.
>
> **Choose customers who pay quickly.** Smart entrepreneurs realize that not all customers are created equal, especially when it comes to how quickly they pay their bills. One business owner realized that he is better off acquiring customers who

pay him lower prices but pay faster—say, in seven days—than do customers who pay higher prices, and are technically more profitable, but pay in forty-five to sixty days. While this might seem counterintuitive, the point, again, is that this entrepreneur realizes the power of capital velocity. He made his money work harder than anyone we had ever seen. By switching from customers who paid him in forty-five days to those who paid him cash on the spot, he saw his margins fall from 10 percent to 7 percent. But he also increased the turn of his cash from eight turns a year to fifty—the total annual margin on his cash went from 60 percent to 350 percent—which meant that he more than quintupled his annual profit dollars with that decision.

Have suppliers fund your business. Your business needs to maximize its potential to generate cash. Sometimes this can mean working with your suppliers so you can pay them in forty-five days rather than thirty to ensure that you have enough cash to cover all of your bills. While this kind of tactic needs to be pre-negotiated with your supplier to make it ethical, it is technically a way to turn your suppliers into your company's de facto bankers.

Negotiate free consigned inventory. This strategy is common in the electronics field. Many distributors, such as Avnet, place inventory of electronic components in the operations of major customers. Once the customers pull the inventory for use, they pay Avnet for the product. This shrinks the inventory exposure to the users and, more important, they keep the cash for product purchases until they absolutely need the items.

If your business is particularly capital intensive—say, a manufacturing operation or steel foundry—you can also work with both your suppliers and your customers to get as near to just-in-time ordering as possible so that you can keep your inventory levels as lean as possible. Another strategy is to get customers to prepay a percentage of a sale as a way to help finance the acquisition of supplies you'll need to complete their order. Whenever possible, you should also lease any capital equipment you'll need rather than purchasing it, if the interest rate is right. Not only can you avoid making a big capital expenditure up front by leasing, it can also be far easier to match up lease payments with the cash flows into your business.

Capital velocity controls your growth rate. Another key point to explore here is the relationship that exists among capital velocity, margin, and speed with which you can grow your company without acquiring external capital, via an investor, for instance. Basically, using these pieces of data you can create an equation that can predict with great accuracy how fast your business can grow before it runs out of money.

Imagine a scenario in which you run a steel business. You have low capital velocity (your customers pay you in sixty days after they receive an order); it's capital intensive (you have lots of equipment and your raw materials are expensive); and, due to heavy competition, your margins are already relatively small. Let's say you have sixty days of accounts payable, sixty days of inventory, and 10 percent gross margins.

Capital velocity = (365/net working capital in days)

Capital velocity = (365/60 inventory + 60 net accounts receivable) = 3 cash turns

Annual Return on working capital = 3 x 10 percent = 30 percent

When you plug those facts into our equation, the truth emerges. You have a very low capital leverage: You turn your money only three times a year and have a 30 percent annual return on working capital. Even when you do turn your money, you don't make a lot. Add that up and it's easy to see that when you grow quickly, you will need additional sources of cash. It's obvious, predictable, and pretty sobering.

A great example to look at is Inspirato, based in Denver, Colorado. They offer luxury vacation homes on beaches, in ski areas, and in desirable cities like New York and Paris. Exclusive Resorts is the innovator behind this model of a premium, membership-based luxury vacation homes business, but there is a key difference: Inspirato rents the homes they use and Exclusive Resorts purchases them! This changes the capital needs and ability to scale and grow massively. Inspirato has the better business model based on capital intensity.

Now, with your Architect hat on, you could try to pull some levers and change the equation, perhaps by working with your customers to get them to pay sooner. Or you could change your expectations for the growth rate of your business, slowing its pace so you can keep up. For example, let's say our fictitious steel manufacturer above improves payment terms from sixty days to thirty days and increases prices 5 percent while also convincing suppliers to offer inventory on consignment where they get paid fifteen days after the product is shipped. With those simple changes, turns improve from three times a year to twenty-four times. Gross margin goes up to 25 percent and generates a return on capital of 600 percent as compared to 30 percent before. That's a twentyfold improvement! It means the business needs less cash or can grow larger without having to go to the market for more capital. If the business could pick customers who paid faster, it could take yet another leap.

This is why understanding the power of capital leverage is a key piece of equipment in any Architect's tool kit.

STRATEGY FOUR: THE MAFIA OFFER
Most of us are not creating new markets out of thin air. We are usually trying to take share from an existing competitor. We do this

mostly because it's a safe bet that any market large enough to go after is being served in some way. So the question is, how do you get those customers to switch over to your product or service instead? And quickly?

Remember the famous line from the classic movie *The Godfather*, when Don Vito Corleone, played by Marlon Brando, tells his godson, the once famous but aging singer Johnny Fontane, that when he talks to the movie director who is refusing to cast Johnny, "[We'll] make him an offer he can't refuse." But did you know that, thanks to some clever insight by entrepreneurial guru Eliyahu Goldratt, our inspiration from chapter one, this same line makes for a great business strategy as well? Let's explore.

First, let's pick on some of the bankers and venture capitalists out there who are always asking entrepreneurs to show them how they can sell into a billion-dollar market. The truth is that if there is a billion-dollar market out there, it's already being served by someone. Unless the market is growing, if you want to build a billion-dollar company of your own, you will always be taking your share from someone else. That's the nature of competition.

The question becomes, how do you set your company apart from your competitors? We find so many business owners who can boast that their product or service is 10 percent better or maybe even 5 percent cheaper than everyone else's, yet their business isn't growing. Why? Because that's still not enough of a difference to convince a potential customer to jump across the moat their current provider has built. The moat is too big. It's too risky to change for only a 10 percent advantage. You'll need to build a bridge.

This is where Goldratt's Mafia Offer comes into play. To truly change your customer's minds—and land them for your business—you need to make them an offer they couldn't possibly refuse. No, we're not talking about sending in a hit man or putting a horse's head in someone's bed like they did in *The Godfather*. Our version of the Mafia

Offer is offering something at least twice as good as what your competitors are offering, or making it available at half the price. While no one is a fan of cutting prices, a price that's half what the competition's asking—particularly if the quality is equally high—will move the market. You cannot make a Mafia Offer by doing things the same way, of course; you will need an innovative offer that costs less to deliver and hopefully yields a better customer experience.

> Our version of the Mafia Offer is offering something at least twice as good as what your competitors are offering, or making it available at half the price.

When you make such an offer to a customer it takes much of the risk out of the equation for them, which is what you need to do to get them to make what could be a painful switch from their current supplier. Think about what T-Mobile is doing when they offer to pay for the cost of breaking a contract from an existing provider when a new customer signs up with them. That's a great bridge over the moat built by competition through the use of contracts.

Consider also what's happened in the large TV market. Just a few years ago, you needed to pay upwards of $5,000 to get a sixty-inch high-definition rear-projection screen. It was worth the cost if you loved watching moves or sporting events. But what do you think happened when plasma and LED alternatives started hitting the market? While their quality was about the same as those rear-projection units, they were available for about $1,500. The end result was that the market for rear-projection units vaporized almost overnight.

Your option in making your customers an offer they couldn't possibly refuse is to make your product or service offering twice as good as anything your competitors can bring to the table. Netflix is a great example of a twice-as-good business model that blew the brick-and-mortar DVD rental model out of the water. Why would anyone continue to go to the store (and possibly wait in a long line, to boot) only to find out the movie you wanted wasn't on the shelf, when you could just go to your computer, organize your personal queue, and then simply open your mailbox a day or so later instead? Not only that, Netflix got rid of late fees and the need to get back into your car again to return the movie. It was a no-brainer choice that was at least twice as good as the current offering.

Of course, Netflix has had to up its game once again now that we can instantly access movies via streaming services as well through Hulu, Amazon, and others. It's no surprise that when we as consumers were given the option of instant gratification when choosing our movies, most of us immediately switched away from the once-innovative mail order business that Netflix had pioneered. Again, online streaming proved to be at least twice as good as the alternatives. Proprietary content is the new frontier on building a moat around on-demand video customers.

To work most effectively, the Mafia Offer needs to be something customers really care about, which means you must understand your customers' needs and wants. Some customers, for example, make their buying decisions solely on price. If those are the type of customers you want to attract, then that's where you need to focus your Mafia Offer. If you run a Motel 6 or a Super 8, you need to offer customers a great discount. But if you run a luxurious hotel in Bali with butler service and individual villas, where your customers are more interested in top-notch care and personal attention than price, your Mafia Offer has to be something unrelated to price. If you made one of these customers an offer to stay the night for $69, they would likely be suspicious about what they were going to get in return. A better offer might be a discounted spa treatment or an upgrade from a basic room to a junior suite.

STRATEGY FIVE: SIMPLE IS HARD

A great quotation attributed to the French mathematician and philosopher Blaise Pascal appears in a letter he wrote in 1657: "I have made this longer than usual because I have not had time to make it shorter." (An English translation of Pascal's *Lettres provinciales* is available at www.arcticbeacon.com.) It has been shortened to: "If I had more time, I would have written a shorter letter."

What Pascal meant, we believe, is that he had simply scribbled down what he was thinking at the time rather than spending the time to plan and process his ideas before he picked up his quill and ink bottle.

Pascal, of course, couldn't edit as easily as we can with the help of our word processing software, so he meandered and digressed as he scratched the words onto his piece of parchment, which resulted in a longer and denser letter than he might have wanted to send.

This exact same thing happens all of the time when it comes to designing our business processes and systems. When we don't do the necessary work upfront to create a design that is simple and elegant, we end up building products and services that are complex and cluttered. We have all experienced processes that touch all the bases, but it is clear that the designer didn't work on making the process efficient and effective. This gets worse over time as we try to account for all of the possible variations in our processes and they get sloppier and slower. Just as our basements and attics accumulate junk over time, so, too, do our business processes.

What Pascal understood is that the simple is hard; it takes real thought and time to get across what you mean using fewer words. We have entered an age of intellectual laziness where data glut prevents us from finding the elegant and simple solution. (You may pick up some supporting ideas on this subject in Joseph McCormack's book *Brief* [Wiley, 2014]).

Great CEOs have also learned that in order to grow, you need to simplify and focus. As an ancient adage puts it, "The man who chases two rabbits catches none." The more you focus and begin to gain recognition for how good you are on the thing you have focused on, the faster you grow.

While it might seem counterintuitive at first, one of the best skills any CEO wearing the Architect hat can hone is the ability to say no to anything that doesn't add value to the business. In fact, your "Don't-Do" list should be ten times as long as your "To-Do" list. We work with one CEO, for example, who is considering entering the residential HVAC market, which is a complex business. But he has also made the decision not to enter the business if he can't develop a simple and elegant business model, one that incorporates a limited inventory and has a compelling offer and simple processes. That's how important simplicity and focus should be for you as the Architect of your company. If you can't do simple, perhaps you shouldn't be in the business.

What defines you as a business leader is what you say no to. So be aggressive in saying no to new initiatives and refocus your team on the core business. Being the best in class with a clear value proposition and well-selected customers will ultimately yield far higher returns over the long run.

One of the highest-value roles a CEO can perform is that of the Architect. Lazy CEOs know that a great business model, with deep moats, strong recurring revenue, great capital velocity, a Mafia Offer, and a simple design, win in the market. Creating such a business is hard work and requires you to say no to a lot of things that seem attractive on the surface but distract from the singularity of purpose. Get the business model right and life will be easy.

KEY POINTS

- Great business models have lots of recurring revenue, high gross margins, low capital requirements, and great return on assets employed.
- The five remodeling strategies are Moat Building, Recurring Revenue, Capital Velocity, Mafia Offers, and Simple Is Hard.
- The six types of moats you can build around your organization are data, network effect, intellectual property, switching-cost, speed, and talent.
- Recurring revenue is a powerful growth strategy: It's easy to grow, fund, and sell.
- The five primary types of recurring revenue are repeat, basic, contracted, sequential and recurring, and recurring with a network effect.
- You can add recurring revenue streams to existing products through service contracts, maintenance, training, financing, and bundling.
- You can make the shift to recurring revenue when you release a new product.
- Capital velocity is a critical factor to growth rate.
- When customer funding is the first choice, customer selection should be based on speed of payment.
- When you want to work your supply chain, the terms of payment control your growth rate.
- Make Mafia Offers—offers so good your customers can't refuse.

- Focus = growth.
- Building simple business models is hard intellectual work and requires saying no to almost everything.

Chapter Four
THE COACH HAT

Selecting the right person for the right job is the largest part of coaching.
—Phil Crosby

What's the job of the coach of a sports team? Recruit great players, coach them, and provide an environment where they can achieve top levels of performance while also expelling those players who don't perform or fit the culture. The job of the Lazy CEO as Coach is exactly the same. Getting the right people in the business, focused properly, with the tools they need, is central to becoming a Lazy CEO, just like Phil Crosby, one of the luminaries in quality consulting, indicates.

It's been our experience at Inc. CEO Project that some hardworking, yet lower-performing CEOs push back at this challenge, saying that duties related to hiring and retention are the domain of human resource experts. True, HR professionals are valuable assets, but spending time on talent acquisition is one of the highest-leverage investments any CEO can make in their business. If you can help your business build a better talent base than any of your competitors, you will establish a significant competitive advantage that can pay dividends for years. That's why it's simply too important a function to delegate to HR. This is the talent moat we discussed in chapter three as one strategy to use while wearing the Architect hat.

To build a high-performing team, you need to first answer questions such as these: "Where are we strong?" "Are we strong in the places that have the most impact?" "What is our strategy, and how does the talent we have enable and accelerate this thrust?" Performing this kind of analysis helps you determine the members you need on the team and what skills they need to bring. These players can either come from within the organization or be recruited from outside.

> Getting the right people in the business, focused properly, with the tools they need, is central to becoming a Lazy CEO.

While Michael Lewis's famous book *Moneyball* (W. W. Norton & Company, 2004) offered a deep look into the analytics behind baseball, the Oakland Athletics' general manager Billy Beane made some very specific decisions about his strategy. He decided that defense in the field was not very important. Rather, he focused on pitching to get outs on defense and on-base percentage for offense. He stood out from his general manager peers in that he did not care how this result was achieved. For example, because you can get on base with a walk or a hit, Beane valued a player who was walked frequently the same as he valued one who hit lots of singles. This approach allowed him to inexpensively find players not valued by other coaches because they didn't fit the traditional models.

As part of their analysis, good general managers, like good CEOs, always start by looking within the organization to ask questions like: Can a player be shifted within the organization—say from first base to the outfield—to meet the need of the team or to make up for a weakness? That assessment also includes determining whether there are any high-potential players in the minor leagues who might be capable of stepping into a key role in "The Bigs."

At the same time, we need to assess our weaknesses and see if we can trade players who don't fit our strategy to other teams who might have a weakness of their own. If, say, we have a slugging left fielder whose poor defense makes him a liability, could we find a way to turn him into an asset by trading him to a team that has a designated hitter slot open? Or it could even involve signing a high-profile free agent to fill a hole on the team. If your team lacks a Gold Glove–caliber center fielder, you may want to invest in acquiring the best one available on the market. But every GM's first choice should be to try and develop a player's skills to make him a better player. The second choice would be to shift him to where his limited ability makes him less of a liability. Finally, you would look to remove that player and replace him with someone from the outside if he remained a liability. These are exactly the same techniques that you as a CEO should use with any of your employees who are not performing: Try to develop them, maybe shift them to another position, and if that doesn't work out, consider releasing them from the organization.

Bringing in external talent is riskier than is relying on internal promotions; even if someone is talented, he or she might not fit into the culture you're trying to build, thus marking that newcomer as a liability. We've all seen late-in-career acquisitions that never fulfill their promise. You pay a lot for free agents based on past performance that they are not able to replicate. Going outside to replace an employee has similar risks. In fact, most research says that this approach has at best a 50 percent probability of success.

That's why all CEOs, like good general managers, need to be personally involved in recruiting A players, from assessing whether they will fit into the culture to then convincing them that joining the team is the best move for them because they can meet their goals of winning a championship with you. Remember, A players want to join the organization because of its vision and mission (great players often take less money for the chance at winning a championship). And, ultimately, the CEO can share that passion and outlook better than anyone else in the organization. When you can acquire the best talent that also fits best within the culture of the team you're building, then you've truly hit a home run, which is why this isn't a job you should entirely hand off to the HR team.

Similarly, your focus should be on building a system within your organization that allows ordinary people to perform extraordinarily. While baseball teams like the New York Yankees and the Los Angeles Dodgers have adopted a strategy of outspending every other team in the league to acquire the most high-profile (and highest-paid) players, the players' performances haven't always matched the investment. And the fact is that few teams or companies can afford to take a similar approach.

> CEOs ... need to be personally involved in recruiting A players, from assessing whether they will fit into the culture to then convincing them that joining the team is the best move for them.

The Kansas City Royals and the Oakland A's, on the other hand, have actually outperformed the Yankees in recent years with far smaller budgets because they have focused more on a system that allows for signing up imperfect and developing players who fit particular roles on their teams. They have done this by employing deep data analytics about what is needed to win baseball games while also taking advantage of inefficiencies in the market. Yes, all things being equal, it's nice to have superstars on your team. But it's far more practical and sustainable to focus on building a system and a strategy that allows everyone on your team to perform like an A player even if they don't have A-caliber talent.

ACQUIRE TOP PERFORMERS AS YOUR COMPANY'S CHIEF TALENT OFFICER

All CEOs need to add another title to their business card: Chief Talent Officer. As we mentioned earlier, acquiring and developing the talent in your organization is far too critical to delegate to HR. The best CEOs, in fact, are always on the lookout for talent, even during meetings and interactions with customers, suppliers, and competitors, even when there might not be a clear opening in the company to fill. Some leaders will hire great talent even if they don't have an open job. This is hiring the athlete and not hiring the position. While that might be counterintuitive, the best CEOs understand that talented people will find their own ways to contribute to the organization. If high performers can't find their niche, they'll leave.

When you do have a particular position in mind and you're bringing on top talent, it's critical to give that person clarity about what you're expecting him to do. That means writing down clear objectives. If you hire a new regional sales manager, for instance, you may want to quantify his goal to be growing sales from $1 million to $3 million over the next eighteen months. This is extremely important because it helps screen out the people who might not be comfortable with shooting for such a goal. High performers actually want to keep score because they expect to meet and perhaps even exceed their goals. These A players are OK with being held accountable because they expect they'll be rewarded if and when they do outperform. C players, on the other hand, get scared off by the idea of meeting highly visible goals, which is wonderful because they prescreen themselves out of your organization.

FINDING THE RIGHT PEOPLE AT THE RIGHT TIME
Firms can afford to attract and retain talent based on the perceived risk and return at each stage of company growth. These stages are

repeated and recognizable, and an appreciation for them will improve your ability as a CEO to act properly at each stage and get the best talent, given your situation.

At the root of this dynamic is the individual assessment of risk and return by the target employee. She will ask herself if she wants to commit her time and energy to your cause and if her returns in the form of compensation, impact, and personal mastery are worth it. Less well-funded start-ups will have to pay for the perceived higher risk taken by the early employees in many forms, such as base, bonus, and equity. People are smart and make personally optimizing choices, balancing risk and return. Later-stage and well-funded firms have an advantage that allows them to pay less equity in recognition for their perceived lower risk.

Early Stage: Bootstrap Start-Up

The typical bootstrap start-up has a core team of one, two, or more founders and shareholders who each bring their talents to the table, generally from functional backgrounds. Some of them may have run larger operations, but more typically, they have specific expertise within a larger firm and do not have exposure to the growth and high-change environment. In the early stages of company growth, their skills are at a premium to do whatever is required to define and execute the business plan. This broad-ranging set of demands on the start-up talent puts value on people with a wide skill set, who are available due to the lure of higher equity compensation and the return if the firm does well. This is particularly true for people who have operated in a lean start-up environment in the past. Many times start-ups are able to afford talent above the level of the market with the same level of direct pay as more established firms. The same job in a larger company would not have an equal level of equity as a start-up, and this allows for the higher initial talent level required to be successful.

As the start-up grows, the jobs of the team change from execution to management of a small group of people, possibly a skill they have from earlier in their career. Performance gaps begin to show at this point, as some of the early team members aren't able to make the change from player to manager. This can also affect the CEO, who normally holds that title but will also handle another job as well in the early days and must change her thinking and actions as she takes on the role of full-time CEO. This is the transition from an entrepreneur to a real CEO. Specifically, the CEO must move some of her work down to the other members of the team so she can take on the longer-range issues now facing the business. If this does not happen, a gap opens with the lack of a forward-looking leader in the business. This leads to slower growth over time.

While not unique to the bootstrap firm, performance issues within the executive team are the domain of the CEO and must be resolved quickly. Friendships and history together can stand in the way of cool-headed analysis and action. Teams must remove this constraint through performance improvement, job splitting, talent shifting, and changing talent; otherwise, the growth of the business will slow and ultimately stop. It can help to review the performance of the top team with an objective external resource such as a trusted board member, coach, or CEO peer group.

As painful as it is, replacing some of original team will allow access to a higher level of talent based on the progress the firm has made along its strategic vision. This, in turn, reduces the risk those new candidates face when they look at the risk-return balance of joining your firm. This talent upgrade can set the stage for the next level of growth.

Early Stage: Well-Funded Start-Up

It is easier to attract talent if the business is well funded. Unfortunately, in taking external equity to reduce the risk of running out of cash, the amount of equity in the hands of the founders has to go down as they share with the new investor. A strong cash position early in the life of a firm is a luxury in the area of recruiting, because the CEO is able to reach into talent pools inaccessible without the lower risk and higher pay this cash can provide. Will a firm with $10 million or $1 million in the bank be able to attract better talent? The normal profile of an executive team for a highly funded start-up would be a set of serial start-up executives, perhaps a group that has done so successfully as a team in the past. Every member would have great skills in their area and a broad business understanding. While bootstrapped start-ups will exchange time for money (taking longer, but with a cheaper solution), the seasoned team does not have patience for this and will exchange money for time, intelligently burning cash faster to get to scale quickly. Since they have done it before, the confidence to make these smart investments frames their decision making.

Middle-Growth Stage
There are two early transitions in how the business operates as it grows based on the span of control. The first transition occurs when the company has about seven people, a team that one person can lead. The communication is direct and clear, and generally the CEO can see every single employee. The second transition occurs when the company has around fifty people, where each of the original seven folks has six or seven people working for them. At this point there will be three tiers in the organization. Communication becomes harder and the lines of sight to results a little less clear. Middle-stage growth happens when you have the fourth level of management.

This stage starts when the company reaches a headcount between two and three hundred, which shifts the nature of the firm and the communication. What worked at a lower scale is no longer good enough. This causes more division of labor and specialization as well as increases the scale and scope of the jobs done by leadership.

Unfortunately, human capacity to perform grows at a different and finite rate in each person, and a rapidly growing firm has the ability to outstrip the existing capacity and the growth ability of all but the best talent. Even if someone is a decent manager of ten people, he or she may not be able to manage a team of fifty.

Spending on organizational and personal development can push the horizon of competency into the future. However, if strong growth continues, almost anyone will become incompetent eventually. The same ideas work: split jobs, shift talent, and change the people. The only way for the CEO to slow this process is to hire above the needed competency for every job as early as possible. This is especially true for the senior executive team where finding the right talent is more important than the direct pay needed to bring them into the firm. Overpaying for the right people is cheap.

But what if the current top leader has reached his or her level of competency? The first challenge is having the personal awareness to understand that the behaviors of the CEO are the limiter in the business. Maturity and insight like this are rare, and input from a CEO peer group or a board is usually needed to help the CEO see the need for change. Second, acknowledging this situation is difficult and sometimes requires incredible emotional maturity so the CEO can take action. If the CEO wants to change, the CEO peer group, a coach, and the board can be helpful in identifying the areas to develop and ways to improve performance. Ultimately, the CEO needs to make a decision about what she desires: going forward within an organization where her performance paces the growth of the firm or bringing in a professional CEO and shifting her position to chairman or owner. No leader wants to step aside, particularly when sitting in the CEO seat of a successful company

Trade-offs of money for time and risk for reward underlie the ability of CEOs to attract the top-flight talent needed to execute their business plan and achieve great results. Understanding the stages of access to human capital and the options available to maximize your team is critical to your CEO success.

SOURCING AND INTERVIEWING

How should you go about identifying the best people to recruit and bring into the organization? Most of the research we've looked at indicates that successful hires generally result from an introduction by someone you know or from someone in your business or personal network. When you rely on a recruiter to find your candidates, your chances of landing a talented contributor fall by about half, especially when it comes to A players. That's particularly troubling, since the cost of making a bad hire, resulting from the money and time invested in bringing them in—especially a senior-level talent—can be crippling to a growing company.

As Chief Talent Officer, you and your executive team can help in this regard by tapping into your own networks via LinkedIn, Facebook, alumni listservs, business and personal networks, and your contact database to get the word out about who you might be looking for. This approach to sourcing talent is effective because you automatically get candidates screened and vetted by your connections who won't be willing to put their own reputations on the line unless they truly believe in the person they send along to you.

You should also distribute a job specification for exactly what you are looking for as far and wide as you can. Included in the job description should be a quantitative description of how the performance will be measured in this role. By providing this clear set of requirements, you will allow your network to find what you want.

The key to this screening process is to identify the people who have the *will* to take on the position—not simply the *skills* to do the job. That's where the interview process comes into play. And the key to interviewing is spending more time assessing every candidate's will and cultural fit than their skills, which should be taken care of through an initial resume- or phone-screening process.

TEAM INTERVIEWING

Determining whether or not a candidate will fit within the organization is also not a one-person task. The most successful interviews are tackled by teams. The idea is to bring a cross-section of the organization together to interact with and assess the person's potential fit within the organizational culture. Each team member then delves into asking questions about a separate area of the candidate's background and talents, thus eliminating the same interview multiple times in a row.

> The key to this screening process is to identify the people who have the *will* to take on the position—not simply the *skills* to do the job.

Ideally, you as Coach and Chief Talent Officer would be a part of that interview team. That's particularly true when you're hiring senior officers and high-impact positions. Not only should you be there to assess the candidate, you're also the best person in the organization to help sell the candidate on the mission and passion of the organization. All too often CEOs delegate this entire phase of the hiring process, not realizing what a powerful influence they can be on the recruitment process. Joel Trammell, founder and CEO of NetQoS, a network performance management business that was once one of the fastest-growing technology firms in the country, is a great example of the CEO as Coach and Chief Talent Officer. He personally interviewed each of the 260 people he had on staff in his business before he eventually sold it (and that doesn't include all of the people he interviewed who they *didn't* hire)!

Trammell told us he felt that this significant investment of his time was justified considering how critical it was to get the right people into his organization. Plus, he added: "I have gotten really good at interviewing. Why wouldn't I do it?" While Joel makes a great point, not every CEO needs to make that same level of commitment. If your firm is hiring thousands of employees, for instance, that simply isn't a feasible strategy. But if your firm is like most of the fast-growth companies out there, you may find that talent is your biggest point of constraint and, thus, worth every minute you invest in bringing the best fits into your organization.

Admittedly, Trammell ran a software company where everyone was a high-level professional, from marketing to sales to engineering. He wasn't hiring minimum wage workers. In other words, his approach might not be as effective for other types of organizations, but it would certainly work for the top two to three hundred people in the organization who likely control the destiny of the business.

BE SURE TO OVER-HIRE

Lots of constraints are actually talent issues in disguise. One of the primary reasons why a company's growth slows is that they run out of the talent they need to keep expanding. But be careful here: You might be retaining an underperformer, thinking you have a systems problem, when it really comes down to the talent. If sales are slumping, for instance, or the quality of your computer code isn't what it used to be, it's possible that you are dealing with a talent issue rather than a process or capital equipment limitation. And a gap in the capability of the middle and front-line management is almost always causing the performance issue because these competencies are the last to develop in a growth company.

This is why the highest-performing organizations consistently over-hire when their growth curve is still on an upward trend. That means targeting people with the skills and experience of running a company twice your size, because those people will already have the experience necessary to answer certain questions related to growth. Hiring people with the skills at the current size might struggle to deal with the changes as the business grows. The friction most organizations run into when thinking and acting like this is that it's expensive; more talented and experienced people cost more. But, as the old adage says, you get what you pay for. As Chief Talent Officer, you may need to make some interesting cost-benefit decisions related to how much your business might be suffering because you're not reaching for the right people, especially in key roles like sales and product development.

EVALUATE YOUR TALENT

Do you have the talent you need to keep your business growing? Everyone might like to think they have the best people working for them. But, sitting down and doing some objective evaluation about the kinds of players you really have inside your company is difficult. And, frankly, most entrepreneurs don't like to do it and aren't very good at it.

In their excellent book *Topgrading (How to Hire, Coach and Keep A Players)* (Pritchett, 2005), Brad Smart and Geoff Smart introduced the idea that every employee is one of three types of players: an A, a B, or a C. Here we will discuss the questions to ask to determine if you have acquired the talent you need to grow your business. Let's start by defining our terms, looking first at a B player as our baseline against which you'll better recognize your A players.

A B player is someone who is successful and completes his job as indicated, on time, every day. These employees *perform to a standard*, and every once in a while they might even surprise you with a breakout performance. They're good, steady workers who get the job done, and you need a ton of them to make your company run. At the same time, you know that you can hire another B player any time you need to at a market rate because there are lots of folks like this in the labor pool. B players are normal.

An A player, on the other hand, is someone who vastly *overperforms* in his or her job, tackling, say, three or four breakthrough projects every year. These employees operate at a completely different level than B players do.

Research shows that in order to recruit or to retain A players in your organization, you need to pay them about 20 percent more than the going market rate. But, in return, A players perform at a rate 70 percent higher than the typical B player, which is a significant return on your investment. This is particularly true when it comes to certain roles in the organization—areas such as computer programming or sales—but it pays to have A players spread throughout the organization.

A C player is someone who *underperforms* on the job. These employees are stretched out in their roles and they continuously miss deadlines and make mistakes. If they are new to their jobs, maybe you give them a break because you see their potential to grow into a B player over time.

As you consider the employees in your organization and evaluate which ones are As, Bs, and Cs, ask the following two questions that great Lazy CEOs use to grade their teams. Be careful here, however. Many CEOs are tempted to rank everyone as an A player and this simply isn't true. All three types of players are distributed across every business, with most people being solid B players.

QUESTION 1: WHAT IF THEY WANT TO LEAVE?
Another way to think about the difference between A and B players is to reflect on what happens if one of those employees decides to leave the organization. If an A player says she is leaving, you'll do whatever you need to keep her, such as giving her more money and more responsibility. With a B player, though, you'll tell yourself, "I hate to lose him, but I know I can replace him."

It's worth noting that since A players are generally confident high performers, you can actually have too many of them on the team, which can become disruptive. That's why when you analyze most firms, you'll find that you'll have about 10 to 20 percent of the team composed of A players, with another 60 to 80 percent made up of B players. That's a healthy mix. Where you need to invest some time is correcting for the remaining team members, your C players.

It comes down to this simple question: If that person were to leave the organization, could you easily replace him or her with someone else? If you can answer, "Absolutely! In fact, we could probably upgrade for that pay level," then you know you have a C player on your hands and you need to let the person go.

QUESTION 2: WHAT IF THE COMPANY DOUBLES?

Another question to ask to help you determine if you have an A, a B, or a C player is this: Would the employee be competent if the company doubled in size? This is particularly useful if you think you have all A players and you cannot identify any weaker performers. The answer regarding the competency of an A player would clearly be "Yes." With a B player, your answer would be "Most likely." With a C player, your answer would be a resounding "No way!"

USE AN EMPLOYEE ASSESSMENT TOOL

Clearly you love the people who both perform and buy into the mission of the organization you've founded. These are the A players and maybe even some of your B players. These are the people you as Coach and Chief Talent Officer have to spend your time and resources on developing and retaining within the organization.

Using our Employee Assessment Tool (see Figure 4.1) you can begin to visualize the folks you want to retain in your organization as well as those for whom you will need to design an exit strategy straightaway.

	Buys Into the Vision?	
High Performer	Yes	No
Yes	Easy-in	Terrorist: culture issue
No	Work with them	Easy-out

Figure 4.1: Employee Assessment Tool

People who both perform poorly and do not fit into the company culture represent more challenging decisions. Consider someone who totally buys into the culture and is someone his peers enjoy working with, but who just can't hit his numbers. Given how difficult we know it can be to find people who fit the organizational culture, this individual represents a good bet to find out if he can be coached and mentored to improve his performance, as long as he also has the will to make the necessary improvements.

As a leader, you must also recognize that perhaps it was never made clear to this person what he needed to do to hit his numbers. Likewise, he might not have the right skill set for his current position, or perhaps the position has grown along with the company and he couldn't grow along with it. These kinds of scenarios present you, as the CEO wearing the Coach hat, with different options. You could break the job up into something smaller that the employee might be able to handle, for example; or you could move him into a new role entirely. Hopefully, by giving this person time to recover, by communicating expectations to him, and by giving him the opportunity to gain new skills or find a position he fits well in, he will see the light in terms of how he can improve his performance in a way that allows him to become a positive contributor to the organization. The rub is that you need to hold him accountable for making that transition. If he can't, then you'll need to make the hard decision to let him go. The truth is you didn't create the problem; this individual did. You're just the bearer of bad news. Your employee will appreciate your honesty and the opportunity you gave him. (We will go into depth on a six-step approach to underperformers later in the chapter.)

The last employee we need to discuss is someone who is a fantastic performer but who doesn't fit into the company culture. Employees like this, to be blunt, are incredibly destructive to every organization they work in. You might call this type of employee a "cultural terrorist." Or a "brilliant jerk." She follows her own rules and is abusive to the rest of the staff. She isn't a nice person to be around. But, again, she's a rainmaker, and that's someone every organization loves to have. In this case, though, you need to go through the same steps you did with your underperformer: You need to communicate what the problem is and offer the kind of coaching that might help her turn her act around. Obviously, you can't make her a nicer person, but perhaps you can make her aware of how damaging her behavior is to her peers and see if she is willing to make changes accordingly. If not, then, just like with your underperformer, you need to show your rainmaker the exit, regardless of how much revenue she generates. These moves make powerful statements to the team about culture—what is tolerated and what is not.

Even after this person leaves, you'll hear stories about how horrible a coworker she was and how your other employees were shocked that you didn't know. That's the kind of risk you face in putting off the hard decisions about your C players. The longer you let them remain, the more damage they cause inside your culture and to your own reputation as a leader. People will lose trust in your abilities, which can undermine all of the hard work you've done to build a strong team in the first place. When you terminate a cultural terrorist's employment, it should be known within the organization that the person is no longer with you because of her behavior, not due to her performance on the job. This will set a tone about the kind of culture you want to build.

ONBOARDING NEW HIRES

Obviously, all of the effort you've invested in bringing the best talent into your organization will be wasted if you don't spend as much, if not more, time and effort on making sure that the support mechanism is in place to help those talented employees blossom to their full potential. While this might seem obvious, it's commonly overlooked or underemphasized in most ordinary organizations. One model that works is called ROAR: recruitment, orientation, activation, and retention. Or, as a firm we know puts it: "Hire Right, Train Right, Treat Right." And, when that doesn't work out, they "Fire Right!" If your company doesn't have a similar model, you need to start immediately to make new investments in your people and the support systems around them.

Think about it this way: Most capital-intensive companies wouldn't think twice about spending 3 to 4 percent of their installed capital base on maintenance of their equipment to ensure that it is running smoothly and efficiently. But if you bring up the notion of spending that same percentage of salary on talent development, many CEOs will start freaking out. But why? You should think about your talent as an asset to your business and, accordingly, continually invest in their development at a rate of 1 to 2 percent of your revenue.

Great CEOs understand they need to keep making investments in their best people both to help drive greater performance and to help ensure that they remain in the organization long term. By continually reinvesting in your people, you can keep ahead of your growth curve and prevent running out of the human capital necessary to continue to turbo-charge your growth.

The most important time frame in this process is the first thirty days of any new hire's experience. What most organizations miss, however, is that if they blow that new hire's first impression of the employer, they've already begun to sow the seeds for losing that person.

That's something Joel Trammell understood well. New hires at NetQoS felt the love on their first day. Everything they needed would be already set up, from a great new computer and their e-mail to their phone and business cards. They would then be introduced to their peers and colleagues, launching the relationships that would support their successful transition to the firm.

> Great CEOs understand they need to keep making investments in their best people both to help drive greater performance and to help ensure that they remain in the organization long term.

MOTIVATE YOUR TOP PERFORMERS

It can be tough to find A players. There might be just 10 to 15 percent of the workforce who can do a job as well as they can at the price you are paying. That's why it's crucial to invest in keeping and motivating your existing star players while also creating an environment that is attractive to other A players. One of the core reasons top performers will stay with your organization is the continuous development of their skills and abilities.

Not all of your top performers are motivated by money alone. In your role as Coach, it's critical to identify what the key drivers are for your top twenty high-performing future leaders, whether that be opportunities to lead, to learn, or to operate autonomously. If you have an aspiring leader who wants to further her education, for example, you could have the company pay for her MBA. What you will find is that doing so will deliver far more value to that individual than if you just gave her the $40,000 tuition fee. When you make the time to understand what motivates each of these individuals, you can build incredible loyalty among them, and you'll get greater performance in return.

External Rewards

When it comes to incentives, using physical items and experiences as rewards can motivate twice their weight in cost. One company we know set ambitious sales goals for the year because they were aiming to improve the valuation of the company ahead of an acquisition. That company's CEO said that if the sales force met their goals, each one of them would receive a Rolex watch. What was amazing is that while a typical Rolex might cost $5,000, the motivation and behavior exhibited by the sales force far exceeded what any $5,000 check would have done. While this was a highly compensated sales force, each making well over $100,000 a year, the team was excited about the challenge and wanted those watches so much, they actually blew past their goals by a mile. Research shows that you can elicit a change in behavior using cash with a minimum of 8 percent of compensation, but you can get the same change with items with a value of 4 percent, so it is worth some creativity in this space.

What adds elegance to these rewards is when the spouse or significant other of the employee knows about the potential reward and will benefit from it. An example here would be a luxurious trip to an exotic vacation if the company's new product is brought in on time and under budget. The spouse will want to go on the trip and thus will become an ally in your cause. When that salesperson comes home every day, her husband might ask, "How are we doing about getting that trip to Cabo?" It's a very powerful way to gather a family together toward a single objective while also smoothing over what could be some long nights or trips away from home leading up to the actual reward.

Another tool for compensating high performers is equity, especially for your best and most valuable performers. Unfortunately, all but the most sophisticated employees will undervalue equity and would rather have cash as an incentive. Our general rule, though, is that in a company's early days, founders should rarely give out equity. Rather, they can use what's known as phantom stock, which is really a share of virtual stock based on the company's value that gives employees the look and feel of equity without actually handing over ownership. This separates the control elements of equity from the cash and income value. You can use such a plan to create what amounts to a long-term incentive plan that is tied to different performance measures of the company—like hitting a certain EBITDA level—after which employees can dip into a pool of money that's been established based on the value of their virtual stock.

This strategy matters because of how difficult it can be to unravel an equity transfer if an employee doesn't work out. Again, when you're dealing with a 50 percent probability of success with every employee you bring in from the outside, it's better to play it safe with something as valuable as equity.

That rule doesn't always apply, however, especially if your company operates in entrepreneurial hotbeds like Silicon Valley, Austin, or Boston, where the best talent expects to receive equity as part of their job. At the very least, you need to have a solid vesting schedule in place as well as rules making it clear that the company has the right of first refusal in buying back any stock if an employee leaves the company.

Internal Rewards

In considering alternatives to motivating top performers with money, it's important to recognize that promoting these A players is not always the best method of developing or rewarding them, either. There are times when some A players are best left in position as strong individual contributors: Think top salespeople or great engineers or software programmers. These are folks who excel at what they do and really have no interest in getting promoted. Smart leaders understand what their A players want and where they can excel. They understand that sometimes no promotion is the best promotion. After all, a worst-case outcome for your business would be to promote an A-caliber salesperson and end up with a B- or C-level sales manager. Instead, you can find ways to offer more complex work, for instance, as a way to motivate these performers.

Another nonmonetary method to drive the performance of A players is summed up by Daniel Pink in his excellent book *Drive* (Riverhead Books, 2009). There, he coins the abbreviation A.P.M., short for Autonomy, Purpose, and Mastery, as the intrinsic rewards that can motivate high performers.

> **Autonomy:** A players enjoy the freedom to get a job done in their own way. So, when you can provide the space in which they create their own accomplishments, it makes their job highly rewarding.
>
> **Purpose:** Work can begin to feel soulless when it consists only of trying to beat the budget numbers from last year. That's why great companies like Medtronic—whose purpose is simply "to extend life"—can attract top talent who want their work to mean something and the place they work to have a higher purpose.
>
> **Mastery:** One of the more underrated elements of creating an attractive environment for A players is giving them the opportunity to master skills they are most interested in, whether it be related to sales, software, marketing, or accounting. The notion

of becoming an expert is highly appealing to A players, and it's something that can also benefit the company over time.

Pink noted that millennials (born between 1980 and 2000) are much more motivated by A.P.M. than by money. So you will need to weave this thinking into your business plans for your talent in this generation.

CULTIVATE TOP PERFORMERS AS YOUR NEXT GENERATION OF LEADERS

You should also be thinking about the kinds of talents you want your team members to develop. Most of us tend to think strictly about individuals and the kinds of skills training they might need or want. But when we start homing in on very specific skills, such as learning a particular programming language or how to use social media for marketing, we tend to overlook some of the real holes in our organization. Usually the largest gap we miss when it comes to developing talent is investing in leadership skills throughout the core of the business. Sure, it's likely you send your most senior level people for some kind of leadership training, but are you doing the same with the middle layer of folks in the organization? If you're not, you're missing a golden opportunity to develop a next generation of leaders who can cut their eyeteeth running small projects and teams and then grow into the kinds of leaders you'll need at the head of your organization as you continue to grow. The lack of middle management is a primary constraint that growing companies face. If you don't invest here, it will show up in slower growth while you struggle to find the leaders you need.

Let's say your organization has a fantastic opportunity to expand into a new city or market. Who are you going to lean on within the organization to take up that challenge? Sure, you could go outside the organization to plug that hole, but you'd have only a 50 percent probability rate of success. You'd be much better off finding someone already within the organization who is ready, willing, and able to take on the position. If you look at organizations that rely on making acquisitions to fuel their growth, you'll notice they aren't as healthy as those organizations that can grow organically. The more you rely on hiring from the outside, the weaker your foundation becomes. That's why it's essential to give opportunities to those already in your tent. But to do that, you will need to make the kinds of investments in talent that will groom the next generation of leaders within your organization.

> The lack of middle management is a primary constraint that growing companies face. If you don't invest here, it will show up in slower growth while you struggle to find the leaders you need.

The objective for the CEO is an excess of talent, a talent-rich environment. This will allow you to find champions naturally and guarantee a group of hungry performers who are always looking for new opportunities to excel. The worst-case scenario is that you cannot absorb all of your most talented employees and they might depart, but they will leave having had a positive experience in your firm and with a set of relationships. Sometimes, top talent is more useful outside the organization!

Your next generation of leaders will be the top performers you want to promote into leadership slots, that is, those who will help drive your organization forward. How do you get this next generation ready for their next role?

Here are a few simple approaches you can use to develop these critical team members.

1. **Educate them.** Sometimes the only thing holding back

an A player is a gap in knowledge. You could help close that gap by, say, paying for an MBA, an advanced engineering course, or even a program focused on managerial skills. Talk to your star performers and find out what drives them and where they want to grow; do this before moving to address any education holes that might be keeping them from reaching those goals.

2. **Increase their scope.** Make your A player's job bigger by expanding the scope or depth of his or her job (which, incidentally, is the opposite of what you do with a C player). If you have men and women you think can become top leaders in time, double or even triple their responsibility within their function in a way that grows their capacity as a leader. For a sales leader, you might expand the size of their region, or increase the number of their direct reports from five to fifteen or twenty. A project manager might move from one to three or four projects.

3. **Increase their breadth.** Whereas depth is digging more deeply into a job function, expanding the breadth means you challenge your A players by cutting across many functions in the organization. If you have star engineers, for instance, ask them to lead a project that also includes marketing, finance, and personnel. It's a great way to grow their knowledge base and their understanding of the business as a whole while also giving them the chance to work with different kinds of people across the organization.

4. **Mentor them.** Pair up each of your A players with a more senior person on the team for conscious mentoring. The

senior person can even be the CEO. The goal is to expose your more junior A players to people in positions you eventually want them to grow into. The process could be as simple as having lunch every few weeks as a way to help build the relationship and begin to open doors in the organization for your rising star. These meetings can also be very valuable for senior leaders, especially CEOs, because it gives them the chance to assess the talent in their organization up close and personally.

When developing your next generation of leaders, think Educate, Depth, Breadth, and Mentoring.

USE YOUR POSITION AS CEO TO DEVELOP POTENTIAL LEADERS IN YOUR BUSINESS

As Chief Talent Officer, you should also personally know the next ten to twenty potential leaders inside your company, which might include levels of the hierarchy one to three levels beneath you. Even if you have to keep track of them via a list on your computer or on a piece of paper inside your desk, you need to keep tabs on these folks so that you'll know who to tap when the opportunity arises.

Just how do you go about getting to know your potential leaders? Informal and formal exposure is a great approach to gauging the talent's strengths and weaknesses and to contribute to their development. This means sitting in their meetings, dropping by their offices for discussions, having an occasional lunch together, and possibly traveling together on an important project. Your ability to personally develop young leaders through sharing your knowledge is invaluable and has a very high impact. You'll be amazed at how these personal relationships improve retention of these top performers.

Embrace Learning Opportunities

Although sending people to class is great, nothing can replace the value of learning on the job itself. If you can give high-potential employees in your marketing department responsibility over a small- to mid-size project, for example, you're giving them the opportunity to stretch their wings and broaden their experience. Based on their performance in that experiment, you can then nudge them into managing multiple projects simultaneously or, better yet, projects that span multiple disciplines throughout the organization. All the while, you'll be incrementally growing their skills and confidence. Most people like to be comfortable, which means swimming in the shallow end of the pool. Your role is to inspire them to go deeper and deeper as they build their new skills and experiences. This is what we mean by keeping people activated and engaged and learning in the business, energies that begin to create bonds of loyalty that will keep your best people in your organization over the long run. How many times have friends told you they left a good firm because they were bored or because they didn't feel connected to the leadership?

As the CEO, you play a key role in this development, since the more your developing leaders feel like you are taking a personal interest in their projects and success, the more they will develop a connection to the organization. That means making yourself available as a Coach to answer questions and to deliver praise and tough love wherever they're appropriate. Your role is to make these people feel loved.

In the end, if you aren't cultivating higher-performing talent throughout every level of your organization, you're likely creating a constraint on the growth curve of the organization as a whole.

Reviews and Rewards

Another commonly overlooked aspect of developing talent is giving people the right kind of feedback and compensation that helps motivate them to continually improve their performance. An example where most ordinary organizations fall down in this regard relates to when and how they conduct reviews of employee performances. We're all familiar with the traditional annual review, of course, but the highest-performing organizations have learned to shorten this cycle considerably, building feedback systems that operate on a monthly or even a weekly basis. The problem of conducting a review every twelve months is that things are forgotten or get lost in the shuffle, patterns get set, and by the time you identify new opportunities or challenges, it's already too late to tackle them. But if you have a much more iterative system, where employees and managers work through issues on a more frequent basis, you can eliminate any surprises by the end of the year.

Think about this as you would if you were coaching your kid's baseball team. Would you wait until the end of the season to give the players feedback on how they hit, fielded, or pitched? Of course not. The idea in putting on your Coach hat is to help ensure that there is constant feedback in your workplace—just like on the baseball diamond—so that every player on your team is delivering the best performance possible while also feeling engaged as part of the team and its future.

This equation also helps explain why it's important to identify underpaid A players in your organization and correct their compensation before it's too late. Another way to look at this scenario is that if you have B players who are paid below market rates, they will begin to accept that they aren't expected to deliver performance relative to the top of the market. The better bet is for you to pay market rates for top performers and for B players, while showing poor performers the door. That's simple behavioral economics at work.

Performance-Based Pay

You should also be weaving variable pay into every position you can. You want your people to be focused on the overall success of the company and to have their upper-end compensation tied to that success. That goes for your line workers all the way up to your executives and sales VPs. The point is to build in what amounts to a bonus system that rewards everyone for the performance of the company beyond what they might earn as an individual. Be careful here that you design a system that compensates for the right behaviors, because if you are paying for a particular behavior, you will get it. If the system compensates for undesirable behaviors, you will quickly need to make changes.

Studies have shown that it takes about an 8 percent change in compensation to change someone's behavior, which can be particularly useful when setting up your variable plans since most companies tend to stick to 3 to 5 percent plans. It's unclear whether or not you could create further gains by going further than 8 percent—to 10 or even 20 percent—but what is clear is that you won't change behavior if you aim too low. Sure, people will be happy to get that extra 3 percent, but it won't change how they behave.

When creating a variable compensation plan remember that you can't treat everyone the same. That would be a mistake. You need to construct the plan so that it sends a clear message about the kind of behavior you want to see continue in the organization and the kind you want to stop. Top performers will get a greater share of the shared bonus.

When it comes to hiring and developing the best talent, there is also a need to consider the best ways to compensate and reward them. Now, as we mentioned in brief earlier, many entrepreneurs can have sticker shock when it comes to paying more for great talent. By most estimates, A players cost about 20 percent more on average than do B or C players. But, and this is where the calculation becomes easy to understand, A players deliver on average 70 percent higher levels of performance than their peers. So, again, you might pay 20 percent more, but you get a 50 percent incremental return that compounds every year! That sounds like a pretty good deal.

Another critical factor in designing variable compensation for your personnel is to ensure that they have a direct line of sight as to how and for what they are getting paid. Salespeople need to know, and be able to do, what they are required to accomplish to get paid. But it's not always as clear-cut for every job function. Sometimes you need to be creative when it comes to other positions: Employing an option such as team-based performance, for example, allows you to pay bonuses based on an entire department or location. Simplicity and clarity should be the guiding principles when designing compensation.

In chapter three, where we discussed the CEO's Architect role, we briefly mentioned the talent moat as a strategy to build a competitive advantage, but the tactical deployment of this strategy actually shows up when you are wearing the Coach hat.

Giving your C players nothing also works at a strategic level. You might find yourself paying your B players at the seventy-fifth percentile range compared to the market, for instance, while paying your A players at the ninetieth percentile and your C players down at the fiftieth percentile. By creating those kinds of thresholds, you make it much harder for your competitors to hire away your best performers. At the same time, you make your weakest performers more willing to choose for themselves to exit the organization.

DEAL WITH OR DIVEST YOURSELF OF UNDERPERFORMERS

One of the most challenging tasks for any leader is figuring out what to do with an underperforming team member, a C player. The challenge is that the C player might be a good person, probably someone who has even bought into the values of your culture. The simple answer is to fire the person and move on, but that isn't the humane way to treat people. On the other hand, he or she isn't performing up to your standard. So what do you do?

Step 1: Make Them Aware There's an Issue

The first step in dealing with underperforming employees is to make them aware that they are underperforming. Simple, right? You need to be as specific as possible about where the individual is falling short, which means it helps to bring data with you to prove your case. It's also something you need to do as soon as you know it's happening, regardless of whether the employee recently joined the company or just had an annual review. The point is that you can't afford to wait until an end-of-year review to let an underperformer know that a problem exists; it needs to happen immediately.

Step 2: Offer Coaching for Improvement

Once you have let your employees know they are underperforming, you can coach them to improve their performance. Before you begin, though, you need these underperforming employees to own the fact that they are falling short in their performance. If you can't break through to them, then your conversation, and their time with the organization, will become very short.

If your employees do own their performance and commit to improving it, then you can work together to put a plan in place to get them up to standard. If the person works in sales, and is only closing five deals a month instead of fifteen or more, you can ask what he or she will do differently to reach that new level. After fifteen days, check in to see what progress has been made, and again after thirty days. If the person isn't on track, then you know you have a problem on your hands and can begin planning your next move.

Step 3: Educate Them

It's possible that your unproductive employees might actually lack the skills they need to perform their jobs well. This could be an opportunity to help them learn those skills that will help elevate their performance. But remember, this is a short-term effort targeted specifically at helping underperforming employees learn the skills to do their jobs better. It's not about offering to pay for them to get an MBA.

Step 4: Shrink the Job

Sometimes, especially in the case of fast-growing companies, employees find that the company's growth outpaces their own ability to keep up. You see that a lot with managers and executives who excel during the early years of a start-up but begin to fall behind as the company continues to scale up. One of the options you can employ to help an underperformer is to break up the job as a way to make it more manageable. Take a sales and marketing leader as an example. Perhaps you could divide up the job into sales and marketing, leaving the incumbent in one of the roles and hiring for the other. While this can often be effective, it also involves someone checking his or her ego at the door to make it work, which isn't always possible.

Step 5: Change the Position

If you have an employee who continues to underperform despite the help of coaching, training, and shrinking the job, you might consider moving the person into a different position in the organization where he or she might be a better fit. Maybe a salesperson would be a better fit in a product support role where he can worry more about helping other salespeople be successful than about filling his own quota. Again, you might encounter ego issues with such a move, so it's advisable to keep that person's salary the same even after the shift as a way to mitigate that. He might not get a raise for a while, but it will help him keep a positive mindset as he attempts to scale up into the new position.

Step 6: Exit Time

If you've done everything possible to put your C player in a position to succeed, without success, then it's time to arrange for that person's exit from the organization. If it comes down to this, you can give your employee the chance to take the soft road out, wherein you give him three months or so to find a new job as a way to avoid terminating him directly. This strategy is generally offered in place of a severance arrangement.

If this approach doesn't work, you'll eventually need to make the hard decision to terminate him with the hope that he'll find a new job soon. Obviously no one likes to terminate anyone. But it's essential for you, as the leader, to remember that your organization can't afford to rely on C players for its future success. Ultimately, the organization is looking at you to be the head coach and make changes on the team if they are needed. If you aren't willing to wear your Coach hat, they might begin to wonder if you aren't a C player yourself.

C players get nothing: no raises, no bonuses, no promotions. That might seem harsh at first glance, but the point is that you are sending a crystal-clear message to that person that he or she should begin pursuing other options. The humane thing to think about when it comes to C players is to be clear with them about their level of performance and why, because of it, they will not be receiving any additional compensation or responsibility. Ideally, this should not surprise them if your management team has been giving regular performance feedback.

Once you reach an understanding with employees at this level, consider coaching them about how they can move themselves out of the organization to find something that will potentially better fit their career paths. There is a school of thought that says everyone can be successful; the challenge is merely to find the job in which that person can excel. And while we like to believe this is true, the perfect job for that C player might not be in your organization. The longer you keep C players around, the more of a disservice you do them because you are playing a role in keeping them from making a productive step in their careers elsewhere. Actively counseling and coaching your C players to find a better fit for their careers is not only better for your organization, it's better for them as well.

REINFORCE THE CULTURE

In their book *Made to Stick* (Random House, 2007), best-selling authors Chip Heath and Dan Heath talk about how powerful stories are to reinforcing cultural values; and that's why you, as Coach of your organization, need to develop a collection of stories that you can use to model the organization's values.

One of the best examples we've heard is still used today throughout the global offices of FedEx. In the early days, the company was trying to make a name for itself by guaranteeing that any package could be delivered just about anywhere overnight. As the company lore goes, one of the drivers was out late one snowy night in the hinterlands of the Midwest to check a drop box for any packages. When he got to the box, the lock was frozen solid and the key broke off in the lock. After trying in vain to reach the packages inside, the driver finally made the decision to drive to a nearby auto garage to borrow a torch, which he then used to cut the legs off the box. The driver loaded the box into his truck and delivered it to the airport where a maintenance team was able to drill it open, remove the packages inside, and get them on the plane to their final destinations. The point of the story, of course, is that it reinforces the message that FedEx will positively do everything it can do to get your package to its destination on time. No amount of corporate slogans is more powerful than this simple story.

Put simply, it is essential for you as Coach of your organization to find stories you can tell to reinforce the values that represent the strength of your culture. That means you should always be looking for stories to reinforce the kinds of behavior you want those in your organization to embrace. Make your employees culture heroes and use their anecdotes to teach how to behave in uncertain situations when they need to rely on company values. It's not enough to plunk down a gigantic rulebook on every employee's desk and expect them to process the contents into meaningful information about how to act or make decisions. In fact, these kinds of rulebooks suck the life and energy out of your A players because they intuitively understand most of what you're aiming at. Don't get us wrong; you need rules in your organization. But it's far more powerful to show them in action, to model them yourself, and to tell stories about people that exemplify the values than it is to insist your staff memorize a tome that doesn't teach them how to handle situations you never thought to include in it.

> It is essential for you as Coach of your organization to find stories you can tell to reinforce the values that represent the strength of your culture.

As a Coach, you should be focused more on reinforcing the values and guiding principles of how you want people to go about doing their jobs. That's where symbols can play an important role. A great example of this comes from the CEO of a hospital who really wanted to reinforce the value of openness and transparency in how he managed. He wanted to share his open-door policy where anyone in the organization could come in and talk to him about issues they might be dealing with. And to do that, he had the doors of his office removed from their hinges and hung up inside the lobby of the hospital, where everyone in the organization could see them and be reminded of his message every day. That's powerful stuff that trumps any e-mail or pamphlet he could have sent out to deliver the same message.

That then begs the question for you, Coach, in terms of what stories and symbols you can share that fulfill a similar mission of reinforcing and communicating culture.

The role of Coach is a primary one for Lazy CEOs. Their goal is to assemble a cadre of highly talented people, motivated and focused on the right issues, with systems to support their efforts. This allows the Lazy CEO to elevate and focus only on constraint identification and elimination, truly working *on* the business rather than *in* the business.

KEY POINTS

- The CEO could be seen as the Coach of a sports team.
- The CEO is the Chief Talent Officer.
- You need and can afford different types of people for different types or stages of a business: bootstrap start-up, well-funded start-up, and middle-growth stage.
- Turn to your personal sources when trying to find great talent.
- Team interview and focus on cultural fit, not skills.
- Over-hire by bringing in talent more capable than you need to enable growth.
- Use the employee assessment tool to separate culture from performance.
- Invest early in development.

- Create focused learning opportunities for high-potential employees.
- Take an active role with high-potential employees.
- Give feedback on performance early and often.
- Performance-based pay is tied to critical performance.
- Non-monetary compensation takes less to motivate change (4 percent of pay rather than 8 percent for money).
- Stories and symbols reinforce the culture more powerfully than PowerPoint presentations and speeches do.
- C players, cultural terrorists, and nonperformers exit stage left.

Chapter Five

THE ENGINEER HAT

Achievement comes to someone when he is able to do great things for himself. Success comes when he empowers followers to do great things with *him. Significance comes when he develops leaders to do great things* for *him, but legacy is created only when a person puts his organization into the position to do great things* without *him.*
—John C. Maxwell

A business is a system for serving customers and making money. And the essential components to any effective system are good processes that deliver these results every time with good people. That means that aligning and improving upon these processes isn't just an exercise—it's absolutely critical to delivering high performance. If you don't have robust processes where it counts, you will be regularly drawn back into the business to deal with system failures. Lazy CEOs don't let that happen twice. Once they deal with the crisis, they put in system improvements and talent to prevent it from happening again. They keep in mind business guru John Maxwell's quotation about putting their organization into a position to do great things *without* the CEO.

A best seller since it was published, and one of the most popular books of all time for entrepreneurs, is Michael Gerber's 1988 classic, *The E Myth* (Ballinger Publishing). Gerber put his finger on many of the key mistakes and motivations business owners should focus on to achieve success. Paramount among his lessons was his notion that to be successful, business owners need to spend far more time working *on* the business rather than working *in* the business. To frame that another way, Gerber tells us that long-term success results from putting processes and systems in place that enable a business to grow beyond the limitations of its people—including the founder and CEO, regardless of how smart he or she might be. This is why the most effective CEOs understand that when they don their Engineer hat, they are looking at the constraints of their business in an entirely new way.

In *The Breakthrough Company* (which I mentioned in chapter two), Keith McFarland calls this "crowning the company." The early stages of growth are led by the energy and vision of the entrepreneur. As the firm matures, the leader must crown the company, which is to place the systems and people of the business first so the leader does not become the constraint to growth.

A classic illustration of the power of systems and processes is Taco Bell. Regardless of whether or not you are a fan of their food, it's nearly impossible not to marvel at the organization. From what started out as a hot dog stand in San Bernardino, California, Taco Bell has grown into a global fast-food giant. For Taco Bell, the workers are truly plug-and-play because the systems they have in place for ordering, cooking, and maintenance are so robust and repeatable that just about any loyal customer can walk into a restaurant anywhere in the world and have products that look and taste exactly the same as what is served in their hometown Taco Bell. This does not mean that the company devalues its employees; quite the contrary. They realize that excellent employees in a great system create a superior result. And they do this with an average turnover in the range of 150 percent a year—that's an entirely new workforce every eight months. Talk about phenomenal process engineering!

Taco Bell discovered that the 20 percent of its locations with the lowest turnover rates enjoy double the sales and 55 percent higher profits than the 20 percent of locations with the highest employee turnover rates do. As a result of this self-examination, Taco Bell has instituted financial and other incentives in order to reverse the cycle of failure that is associated with poor employee selection, subpar training, low pay, and high turnover, taking a processed-based approach to the issue of talent turnover.

This process-obsessed quick-service restaurant recently took another look at their engagement with customers and found that their extensive menu was intimidating to drive-through clients. The time pressure to make a selection quickly and to place an order to avoid holding up the line caused most customers to select simple and lower-value meals. Taco Bell made a small process change in the script for the attendant taking the orders to: "Welcome to Taco Bell. Take your time and let me know when you are ready to order." This took the time pressure off the client to read their large menu and dramatically increased the average order size, thus increasing profits on the drive-through orders. According to the 1994 *Harvard Business Review* article "Putting the Service-Profit Chain to Work" (coauthored by James L. Heskett, Thomas O. Jones, Gary W. Loveman, W. Earl Sasser Jr., and Leonard A. Schlesinger), using the Engineer hat means you are seeking this kind of impactful process improvement that lifts the performance of the entire organization. Even though this article is more than twenty years old, the underlying concept is nonetheless strong and useful.

YOU CAN'T IMPROVE WHAT YOU DON'T MEASURE

Before you progress into the Engineer role, you have to be confident in your measurement system. If you do not have a clear set of metrics that align to your business objectives, your management conversations will be based on theory and opinion. Great companies manage and decide using data.

Financial data are always high on the list; revenue, profits, margins are critically important and the stuff of every management conversation. Unfortunately, these are backward-looking objectives that depend more on the outcome of doing the right things and doing them well. They don't tell you if your strategy is on track. Use financial information, but realize it is an incomplete picture.

Strategic measures that correlate to the basis of competition you have selected are more useful. For example, a customer-service-focused competitor would want plenty of customer feedback data—rankings on how those customers enjoyed the service, speed of service data, and the like. An innovation competitor might be more interested in how far ahead they are of the competition, their innovation pipeline, what percentage of business comes from new products, and the time to profitability of new service launches.

One software business we are familiar with, for example, was trying to penetrate a new geographic area. As one of their top metrics, they looked at sales of any size in that target area. While the total revenue was inconsequential, the movement of customers who purchased product for the first time grew and grew. The team knew that any one customer purchase led to repeated purchases by customers, which was an ideal way to grow the new area.

You need only look to the great retailer Nordstrom for inspiration on how to do this. Every day Nordstrom posts a list of the top ten salespeople in the company; everyone knows who the rainmakers are. But just as important, the company also publishes the letters from customers who are saluting those employees who stood out in supporting the company's mission, which is to "provide outstanding service every day, one customer at a time." Seeing those letters every day is a way to measure how well Nordstrom is tracking to its mission.

One day, for instance, the company posted the letter from a customer who couldn't believe how, after she called a store to see if they had found a diamond that had fallen out of her engagement ring, the staff at the store scoured every inch of floor looking for it. More incredibly, they also went through every dirty vacuum bag until they found it. How's *that* for a clear connection to their competitive advantage?

WHAT ARE THE ELEMENTS OF A BUSINESS SYSTEM?

Business systems are comprised of a number of components that combine to create the system, the "How" for the organization. Those four components are: (1) business rules; (2) information technology (IT) systems; (3) training; and (4) company values and culture. While many leaders think only about IT when a conversation turns to systems, the other three components can have a greater impact on business performance and so they need to be managed just as carefully and strategically as IT.

NAIL DOWN YOUR BUSINESS RULES

One of the critical elements of any businesses system is its set of business rules, which define what we are, what we aren't, and how we do things. While these rules help us understand what we are going to say yes to, they also help us define when we, as an organization, should say no. Southwest Airlines is a classic example. They have a clear vision as a low-cost operator with simple systems. So when one of the executives suggested adding first-class service as a way to generate additional revenue and profits, it was turned down. Why? Because in analyzing the suggestion, they realized that they would be left with empty seats and a more complicated reservation system and boarding process. In other words, it would go against every business rule they had in trying to be the low-cost operator.

Most businesses run their operations with *implicit* business rules, which are developed over time through good and bad experiences. But great CEOs have learned that they need to make their company's business rules *explicit* so that they are highly visible, understood, transmitted, and challenged across the organization. One such example is Homes of Hope, affiliated with the international Christian nonprofit Youth With A Mission, which builds houses in Mexico. That organization's primary fund-raising mechanism is charging fees for building houses. But in 2009, as a result of the Great Recession and other factors that included violence in the country and the fear of a SARS virus outbreak, the demand for missionaries to build new houses dropped precipitously, which put the Homes of Hope's viability at risk. They attributed their survival of this catastrophic drop in revenue to the fact that they had not taken on debt to pay for their buildings, land, and other facilities.

> Great CEOs have learned that they need to make their company's business rules *explicit* so that they are highly visible, understood, transmitted, and challenged across the organization.

Many years later, when one of the organization's members suggested they take on debt to build a new facility, the idea was rejected outright. Why? Because the organization's other members had believed that debt would have sunk the organization in the prior crisis and had thus put a business rule in place stating they would never again take on a mortgage to construct a building, even though they could easily afford it in the current environment.

The implicit rules that drive the business need to be explored, defined, and written down. Once they are cataloged, they are made explicit by being clearly communicated throughout the organization. One way to communicate the business rules is to write them down as operating principles of the organization and to incorporate them into the standard operating procedures. But perhaps still more powerful is to make the story demonstrating the need for the business rule a part of the company narrative. We will talk more about the power of stories in managing culture later in the chapter.

You need to ask what significant business rules you have in place that will define what you will or won't do. Then, from an Engineer's point of view, you have two opportunities:

1. Challenge those business rules with a view toward opening up new opportunities because those rules are outdated or shortsighted. Be aggressive here; sacred cows make the best hamburgers.

2. As you identify opportunities for improvement in the organization, you can also look to make a permanent business rule around one of those improvements. One example is the rule that expense reports must be turned in within two months of the travel date, a rule created when an employee submitted a massive expense report several months late.

GET THE MOST OUT OF YOUR IT SYSTEMS

For any twenty-first-century organization, embracing IT is no longer an option; it's a given. Everyone from solo operators and mom-and-pop shops to Fortune 500 organizations rely on some level of IT, even if it's just e-mail and a website. IT is critical to every organization's success. Only the smartest CEOs also know how to put IT into context, which allows them to spend intelligently to get the maximum return for this investment.

Any IT system generally has two sides: the infrastructure and the applications, all of which sit on the network of hardware. Infrastructure includes your e-mail server, security, storage, networking hubs, and, of course, your laptops and devices; the applications are the systems that run on that infrastructure, including your accounting package, inventory system, point of sale, and customer relationship management systems, etc.

What the best organizations have come to realize is that the CEO, wearing the Engineer hat, should *always* think more about the applications and less about the hardware and infrastructure. Think about your IT infrastructure as a public utility such as water: You should be able to turn it on and have it work. As CEO, you can't add any value here. Leave that to the technicians or to an outsourced organization with deep expertise and just manage the cost of the outsourcing and the service level they provide. Do not dive into details. As Jack Welch once said, "Everyone's back office is someone else's front office." If you don't make money on your e-mail system, it's a back-office process and you cannot hope to be global class in that area. Consider something like e-mail: Why would you manage that in-house when there are clearly organizations that have the scale, capabilities, and expertise you don't have? Your time is best spent finding the different ways you can focus your company's applications to maximize the value proposition you have made to your customers.

In his book *Dealing with Darwin* (Portfolio, 2005), Geoffrey Moore had a useful definition when discussing innovation that applies here: "Core are things that your customers pay you to do. Everything else you do is Context." Many of your applications are Core, since that is what releases value for the customers and hence the organization. Infrastructure is Context.

One way you can kick off that process is by encouraging your IT team to ditch the updates on server speed or e-mail redundancy—those should be automatic—and come up with two to three projects every year that will improve your company's competitive edge with customers in some way that remains aligned with your basis of competition. Ask them what things they can do to help make your customers crazy happy as a result of something the company has done with its applications. A friend of mine recently shared his experiences in staying at Four Seasons hotels. He travels a lot and regularly stays at this particular luxury hotel. He used the points he accumulated in doing so for a trip to Hawaii to stay in a Four Seasons property. When he arrived, he was greeted at the front desk by name, as were his wife, children, and dog! Staff then took him to his suite where there was a dog bowl and custom dog treats for his pet. They continued to surprise the family with special treats that were customized to their tastes. Realize, this was not the hotel location my friend frequented; it was the same organization, but almost 5,000 miles away.

While impressive as a customer service story, this is a more impressive process-engineering story. Clearly, Four Seasons uses their applications to capture information about each of their heavy users and shares it across the organization. That allows them to provide amazing *customer intimate* experiences, supported by their IT. They truly understand the power of their applications.

But a word of caution: Don't make the mistake of thinking that IT is some kind of solution all by itself. You can't just drop IT into something and expect it to solve the issue, though companies do this all of the time. The point about IT is that it should be used as a way to refine and automate the systems and processes in your company that drive value for your customers. If you have a crummy process, adding IT to it won't make it less crummy; you'll simply create a bigger and more automated and expensive mess. To put that another way, the best place to start your next big IT project is to rethink the processes and systems that it will support. Get those right first; then enable them with IT.

TRANSFORM YOUR APPROACH TO TRAINING

The third component of a great business system is training, which you can think of as software for the people in your organization. In other words, if you want people to act and perform in a certain way most of the time, training serves as a kind of software to help set expectations and give them guidance on how to perform. This is normally embodied in the standard operating procedures. The issue is making sure that everyone understands and lives these refined and optimized approaches.

Training is particularly important in organizations where there is significant interface with customers. Think retail, hospitality, and tele-sales. We've all had an experience, for instance, when we've talked to someone on the phone who was clearly using a script. While this can feel impersonal at times, it's also an approach that organizations have devised to try and ensure that they get the best results from the time you are on the phone. The best firms combine structure around the call and allow the operators to use their judgment to make the interaction more human. The measurement systems will provide feedback if their approach is working better than the base methods. Many organizations use this approach to engage the collective mind to make process improvements. When one team member has made a change to the standard approach that shows powerful results, the organizations are quick to capture it and transmit the new way through a change to the operating system.

Training is a powerful approach when the customer interaction is relatively defined, predictable. If customers call with a number of standard requests, or order from a limited menu, training and procedures are in order. Specific stimulus yields a specific response—and an optimized one based on the business objectives. These kinds of interactions are the best ones to automate because they are perfect jobs for computers and really bad jobs for humans.

Unluckily, many customer interactions are not predictable.

The other side of human software is to clearly define the organization's values. The truth is that regardless of how good your training program is you'll never be able to anticipate every possible situation that will occur. That's why the values you transmit throughout the organization are like software that allows people to make decisions on their own. A great story along these lines comes from the Connecticut supermarket chain Stew Leonard's, which has a clear set of values. The Stew Leonard's culture is built around an acronym for S.T.E.W:

Satisfy the customer.

Work together as a **Team**.

Strive for **Excellence** in everything you do.

Get the customer to say **WOW!**

To help support these values, every employee of every store is empowered to spend up to $500 of company money on their own to make something better for a customer. This doesn't happen often, but when it does, it clearly generates a Wow! experience for the customer on the receiving end. And that customer will become a loyal fan of the store and likely spread the word to friends and family.

The company tells an old story about an employee who worked in the lost and found department at Stew Leonard's. A woman walked in looking for a lost gold Cross pen her deceased father had given her. The young employee searched his boxes and the entire store looking for the pen, to no avail. He came back to report the sad news to the woman. He gave her $60 in gift certificates in an era when Cross pens cost around $20, telling her that they couldn't find the pen, but perhaps this would make her feel a little better. When Stew Leonard himself heard about this story, he celebrated it and rewarded the young employee with an expensive external training program.

FOCUS ON COMPANY VALUES AND CULTURE FOR EVERYTHING ELSE
It is impossible to define every situation that might happen in the operation of a business. Business rules will cover plenty of the defined situations. The important and well-known rules will be embodied in the IT systems, and training will take care of the softer skills with human involvement. Even then, there will be scenarios that no one ever imagined. What to do?

This is when the company's culture and values come into play. They provide the guideposts when the situation is uncertain and the rules don't apply. One of our favorites is from Ritz-Carlton's mission statement: "Ladies and Gentlemen serving Ladies and Gentlemen." Simple and powerful, it guides what an employee should do in many situations. Does the Ritz-Carlton need to tell employees to say "Hello" in the morning? No, because ladies and gentlemen say "Hello." Do they need to tell employees to open doors for people? Nope. You get the idea. The concept that any behaviors would be run against the standard of what a lady or a gentleman would do allows them to operate without rigid rules and still make great decisions and deliver superior service. Clear values are particularly important for larger and distributed organizations where access to management or other input might be untimely or hard to get.

The Boy Scouts have a strong set of values called the Scout Law. Boy Scouts around the world recite these twelve attributes at every meeting: Trustworthy, Loyal, Helpful, Friendly, Courteous, Kind, Obedient, Cheerful, Thrifty, Brave, Clean, and Reverent. These are the values that all Scouts aspire to live by. When faced with an uncertain situation, they refer to these laws and then determine what to do. Any organization can build lasting values into their business and use them to guide decision making when the rulebook doesn't apply.

One firm we know of in the quick-serve restaurant space has made it simple: "CCC"—Cheerful, Complete, and Clean. They want their employees to be cheerful when engaging guests, their orders to be complete (the largest point of customer dissatisfaction), and the environment to be clean. It is simple, it is memorable, and it drives local performance.

SYSTEMS ALIGN TO VALUE PROPOSITION

In your role as Engineer, your goal should be to construct processes and systems within your business that most closely align with the primary value proposition you offer your customers on price, customer intimacy, or innovation. If you are competing on price and attempting to establish yourself as the low-cost manufacturer in your industry, the systems you construct within your business should be designed with the idea of how to take as many extra pennies out of your production process as possible, or at least to alert you when a variation occurs so you can fix it. Again, you need systems that can help you ensure that your production process keeps your own costs as low as possible. This will be reflected in your business rules, for example, by what features you need to add; in your IT systems by how you manage your costs; and in training by driving efficiency and process improvements.

If, on the other hand, your customer value proposition is built around delivering a high degree of customer intimacy—where you are offering your customers an incredible experience such as my friend had at a Four Seasons in Hawaii—your systems need to deliver something altogether different. In this case, your goal should be to implement systems that deliver a Wow! experience to your customers, such as remembering that she likes feather pillows and Starbucks coffee in the morning along with the latest edition of the *Wall Street Journal*. Hospitality companies deliver these kinds of experiences with the help of their IT systems because it's simply too much information for humans to remember.

The training the company invests in is also apparent when you pull up at any Ritz-Carlton. That's because the bellhop who helps you remove your bags from your car and checks the name tags is also talking into a two-way radio—"Good afternoon, Mr. Schleckser"—thus alerting the front desk that you will soon be walking into the lobby and ready to check in. The first few times this happened to me, I didn't notice them using this simple system, but I was thrilled to be greeted by name when I arrived.

When it comes to building systems that deliver innovation, you could look at the example of 3M, which not only encourages its engineers to spend 10 percent of their time dreaming up new breakthrough products but also has created a system that brings its customers into the innovation cycle as a way to dream up the kinds of products they need the most. These are excellent examples of business rules that drive systems and alignment with a company's value proposition. And part of the value of that system is that it helps generate, track, and develop the kinds of new value-added ideas the company's customers expect.

But there is a simple idea that people miss all of the time when it comes to pitching their own Mafia Offer, a concept we introduced in chapter three about wearing your Architect hat: It needs to be something that the customers you want the most care about the most. We need just lean back on the work of Michael Treacy and Fred Wiersema in their book *The Discipline of Market Leaders* (Basic Books, 1995) to know that every business competes on three basic levels: cost, customer intimacy, and innovation. To make the best

Mafia Offer, therefore, you need to be clear about which one of these three elements you're basing your competitive advantage on.

Many entrepreneurs would probably try to compete on all three elements. They are blessed with mindsets that see endless possibilities and thus have trouble saying anything except, "Yes!" I've talked to numerous entrepreneurs and asked them which value proposition they were chasing, and more often than not their answer has been, "All of them!" It is impossible to be excellent at three fundamentally different approaches to competitive advantage at the same time. You will inevitably be trumped by a firm that focuses on only one, so you have to pick to be great.

ENGINEERING "WOW!"

By building the right kinds of systems, you can also surprise your customers by delivering on your value proposition in a new and unexpected way. But to do that, you need to first identify ways to exceed what your customers actually expect and make sure you deliver that as a way to avoid disappointment. If you run a car dealership, for example, you need to ensure that your customers' minimum needs are met, such as making sure the repairs are actually done, that costs are transparent, the bathroom is clean, trash cans are emptied, and there's coffee in the waiting room. If you don't do the promised repair, you've failed to deliver on your basic promise to your customers. It won't matter that you washed their cars afterward; it's inexcusable, and you're likely to lose your customers as a result.

Let's assume that you fulfill all of your customers' basic needs and then use systems to deliver something beyond that to create a true Wow! moment, something your customers didn't expect. Think about how the process of renting a car has changed. It used to be you'd show up at the rental agency and, after waiting in line for many minutes, fill out paperwork—sometimes in duplicate—before you could get your keys and drive off. Of course, you had to do everything in reverse when you returned the car. It was a long process that could be made much worse if you were already anxious about being late for your flight. But car rental companies learned that by automating their systems and stepping up training they could actually delight their customers with quick check-in while also improving error rates and reducing costs.

Today renting a car can almost be described as hassle-free and painless. If you have a reservation, your car is usually readied in advance of your arrival. And returning the car is even simpler because attendants can print out receipts within seconds of you parking your vehicle. Now the folks at Enterprise and Hertz need to come up with a new way to generate the Wow! experience because, the traveling public has come to expect a technology-powered car rental experience.

The key takeaway here is that you can align systems with your promise to your customers, and in doing so, you can create a competitive advantage.

THE PAYOFF: SCALING UP

Another huge payoff that results from investing in systems is that it can help your business scale larger. Many entrepreneurs miss this angle. They feel their time is better spent closing sales, making products, or hiring their next executive. While those tasks to undertake—and hats to wear—are important at various times, the truth is that investing in building the systems will enable your organization to blow past limitations you might inadvertently be placing on its full potential. It is, unfortunately, a bit boring to tackle this investment, so many entrepreneurs don't spend time in this role until it's too late.

A classic example of this lack of investment is the decision by most small businesses—and even many larger ones—to rely on Intuit's Quickbooks software to keep their financials organized. We don't mean to knock Quickbooks; it's great for a start-up or small business, but it's just not designed to run a sophisticated company. We've seen companies with revenues of $60 million still tracking their accounts with Quickbooks—not a great idea. What these companies soon find is that in putting off the investment in a more appropriate accounting software solution, they run into problems and errors that become distracting enough to stall growth until they make time and money available to correct the issue. Again, the point is that systems should be in place to fuel your growth, not inhibit it. In the example above, a poor accounting system can slow growth because management will lack the information and analysis needed to make good decisions.

> The smartest CEOs are always thinking about the best way they can invest in systems for the future.

The smartest CEOs are always thinking about the best way they can invest in systems for the future. Think about it like over-clubbing on the golf course. If the shot calls for a seven iron, go with a six iron, something that without a doubt will get you to the green and beyond. That means that if your company is growing into a $30 million organization, you should be thinking of how to build a system that can sustain a $100 million enterprise.

It's possible, of course, to go too far with this way of thinking by putting in new business rules, a massive, complicated IT system, and beefed-up training before they are needed, which will choke the company as it tries to grow. Doing so would be akin to using a long distance fairway wood for a short approach shot to the green. On the flip side, we also understand how you want to conserve your capital, but this isn't the place to go cheap, not when your future growth is at stake. Rather, think about it as making a down payment on your long-term success—where you're putting in place the kinds of systems your team will grow into over time instead of having to wait until the systems catch up with their pace. This is like picking the perfect club, lightening your swing, and landing the ball two feet from the hole.

PICKING UP SPEED

When it comes to assessing the effectiveness of your processes and systems, the most important measurement is cycle time, or the speed at which a process is executed. We discussed this briefly in chapter one, but we need to go a bit deeper on this critical topic. Being fast as a company is actually a huge competitive advantage. Remember one of our favorite adages about being big versus being fast: "It's not the big that eat the small; it's the fast that eat the slow." Think about your business and everything involved in running it. What if you looked at all of those processes and the time they take to complete, and then cut them in half? What would that mean to your competitiveness?

Let's say you have a sale process in place that tracks the time between when a potential customer is first contacted to the point at which you actually collect revenue from them. Clearly, the faster a customer moves through this process, the more effective and beneficial to your company it becomes. Turning contacts into paying customers in three months instead of six is something that improves cash flow, growth, capital velocity, and profits—hopefully before your competition even knows the prospective customer is shopping. Similarly, if you manufacture products, the more streamlined you can make that process—getting products out the door in two days, say, instead of two weeks (particularly if customers really care about delivery speed), the more of a lead over competition you can reap—and you will also lower your costs. A rapid product development process, particularly one that is faster than the competition, is a huge reason why customers will pick your firm as their supplier.

But, again, a word of caution: Speed *is not* the end goal in itself. Your goal should be to speed up the processes that will deliver the most value to your customers based on your promise to them. And, just as important, your goal in making improvements should be to create those extra and unexpected benefits for those customers that value that benefit. You can get there two ways: first, by selecting clients that care about what you are good at; or second, by becoming good at what a lot of customers value. This is an important point because it's easy to get distracted with the notion of "speeding things up" while also forgetting that your customer not only doesn't care about that particular change but also won't pay an extra nickel for it. In this "no wait" society of ours, delivery and speed of service are generally productive areas to spend time on. It's obvious what your customers will choose if you offer them the option of getting their cable television installed tomorrow versus sometime next week. And robust systems are a strong tool in delivering on these kinds of promises. An Engineer could also see to it that people are on the phone calling customers after the bills go out to make sure that there are no discrepancies which might hold up payment, as opposed to waiting until a payment is late before starting an inquiry.

(Note that the ultimate competitive advantage lies in your entire organization wearing the Learner hat. As the tempo of market changes increases, the organizations that learn and adapt quickly will overtake their competitors. This need for rapid organizational learning puts an exclamation point on how important it is for you to model Learner behavior for your organization.)

When you put on your Engineer hat, it's critical to keep your customer at the top of your mind as you build and enhance your processes.

STREAMLINING THROUGH "STAPLING"

In their *Harvard Business Review* article called "Staple Yourself to an Order" (July-August 2004), Benson P. Shapiro, V. Kasturi Rangan, and John Sviokla introduced a concept that lends itself extremely well to CEOs who are wearing their Engineer hats. Namely, to best serve your customers you should, in a manner of speaking, "staple" yourself to them so you could essentially walk through the same experience they would. That way, you would have firsthand knowledge of how best to improve that experience. As leaders, we don't get the same level of service as a normal customer does. It's similar to how staff at a restaurant would be on their best behavior trying to impress a visiting food critic.

> To best serve your customers... "staple" yourself to them so you could essentially walk through the same experience they would. That way, you would have firsthand knowledge of how best to improve that experience.

Think about that for second. How quickly would you have solved the hassles of renting a car or checking into your hotel if you were forced to go through the same pains as your customers do? But this experience can also apply to your customers who order from your website, where you can do things like track how many clicks it takes them to place an order and how long it takes and how many times they may have to enter their personal information. You can almost hear your customers complaining, "I have to enter my address *again*?" While the process of stapling yourself to your customers will no doubt prove to be a painful experience for you, it can also result in some of your biggest and most valuable insights into how you can reengineer the waste out of your systems and processes.

When it comes to removing waste from a system, we can learn a lot from Japanese companies, like Toyota (mentioned in chapter one), that have made efficiency practically a religion. What Eiji Toyoda realized when he developed the Toyota Production System (TPS) was that when you look at an order as it flows through the operation—by stapling yourself to it—you can see and analyze all of the different handoffs and stopping points that the order makes along its journey and finally to the customer. By looking at a process in this way, you begin to see all of the waste created, especially anytime something or someone has to move or you have to redo something. You will also begin to recognize the waste from Time, Inventory, Motion, Waiting, Over-Processing, Over-Production, and Defects, all of which should be targets for elimination as you look to reengineer the system to be as efficient as possible. The following table (Figure 5.1) defines each of the seven wastes identified in the TPS:

Time	Does a process need to be done? Will eliminating it decrease the value to the customer?
Inventory	Holding an asset—waiting for it to go into service, material, money, or talent.
Motion	The physical movement of product or people—bring the process to the person; as well as exchanges between people, processes, or systems.
Waiting	Anytime that value is not being added is waiting.
Over-Processing	Doing more work than is needed, such as doing something twice, like entering the same data more than once on a website.
Over-Production	Making more than is needed for the moment, usually in the name of efficiency.
Defects	Mistakes that cause you to work on something a second time.

Figure 5.1 The seven wastes—TIMWOOD—identified by Toyota

Think about this: We generally organize our systems and processes around functions rather than around customers or orders.

That results in inefficiencies because the process has to stop as it gets handed off to another group within the organization. If you could reengineer that process so that a single group has everything it needs to deliver value to your customer, you'll likely find a way to create significant value for that customer while also shaving your process time significantly. Eliminating those handoffs also reduces the risk of error and the need to redo tasks, both of which are hugely valuable to the organization and the customer.

MEASURING TO IMPROVE

It's a well-known adage in the process improvement space that what you measure you can improve. But many average-performing companies have unmeasured and unmonitored systems that are ineffective. Earlier in this chapter, for instance, we talked about how there are times when you can make a Mafia Offer to your clients, an offer they can't refuse. The question you can then ask when you have your Engineer hat on is, how well is that offer working?

Too often, the Mafia Offers that companies come up with just don't connect with a real need on the part of the customer. But if you design your offers well—a high-leverage task to undertake—you can examine your sales funnel to see how effective it has become. Visualize a funnel, which is wide at the top and narrow at the bottom. You can apply this analogy to your sales cycle by thinking that you talk to a lot of potential customers, but only a few make it all the way through and out the bottom. Obviously, the more customers who flow through the funnel, with high yields at each stage, the more effective your sales process will be.

If you notice that your conversion rate from the top all the way through to the bottom is quite low, then you have opportunities to test ways to tighten up your offer to your customers. Direct mail companies like Publishers Clearing House are masters at engineering their direct response sales process. They use such database sales and marketing techniques as investing huge amounts of time, testing what images and offers—a white colonial house versus a yellow Cape Cod cottage, a red Jaguar versus a silver Porsche—to see what will resonate most with their potential customers and drive up response rates. They run these tests constantly on a portion of their mailing list, say 50,000 people, and then measure the impact of the different approaches. Key here is that they don't make a change unless it is supported with data. Opinions don't count.

We know of a large home security systems company that does massive amounts of analytic marketing. They constantly refine their offers to homeowners, both online and through direct mail, by changing everything from the type of house in the ad to the size of the sign to how many family members it depicts until they begin to see traction. They're never satisfied, always feeling like they can get more traction based on the changes they make to their ads and offers—but only those offers proven to drive up response rates get used. Numbers rule. By conducting even small A/B tests like this to see what variables might have an impact on your customer conversion rate, you can then have significant positive impacts all the way through your organization.

SPEED IN PRODUCT DEVELOPMENT

Another example of this kind of reengineering has been labeled the "minimum viable product," or MVP, which is based on the similar idea of releasing products to get feedback from the market as often as possible. This notion, championed in Silicon Valley, runs counter to how most people think. "Let's make sure we get the product as perfect as possible before we release it" is a more common thought than the one that says, "Let's release enough of a product to see what our customers think so we can make improvements they actually want." As the old saying puts it, "Perfect is the enemy of good." Realize that this thinking is contrary to normal engineering approaches and you will have to educate your development team on why MVP is a better approach.

The point is that software engineers should be thinking of releasing version 0.1 instead of a full-featured version 1.0 in which product managers or the marketing department have defined the needs. The goal should be to start small and go through eighty-nine incremental releases as you build toward that full-featured version 1.0 release. We have seen some firms that never actually get to the fully envisioned product, but they create a strong and viable business on their march toward the ideal offering. This approach is so effective because it provides multiple opportunities to see what works in the market and what features resonate most with customers. It's also a way to create early revenue opportunities, which can be critical if a company is funded externally. And it's a great way to refine your Mafia Offer as you build up to the one pitch that your customers can't help but accept.

This MVP method works particularly well when it comes to innovating new products where the time to market can be cut in half and you get customer feedback much more quickly than under traditional development models. The first iPod, for example, looks nothing like the current offerings.

PLAYING YOUR CARDS RIGHT

Be careful: The broader the top of your sales funnel, the more inefficient you can become. "Overspraying" can be a trap. You can find yourself talking to far too many people who can never be persuaded to become your customer. But salespeople hate to say no to potential customers, orders, and commissions. As a result, they cast as wide a net as possible to find new clients and revenue, wasting company resources in a low-probability effort. The ideal scenario would be to find ways to apply business rules and analytics to help you assess upfront who your most likely potential customers might be.

Performing upfront analysis can be particularly valuable in a sector like government contracting, for example, where it can cost a firm upwards of $1,000,000 just to prepare a request for proposal (RFP)! Clearly, few firms can afford to miss many bids based on that kind of investment. The best firms, therefore, have constructed predictive models based on how they answer thirty questions or so. Things like: "Have we done business with this firm before?" Or, "Did we help write the specification for the job?" Or, "Have we done this kind of work before?" The answers to these types of questions give them a sense of whether they have a 20 percent chance or a 70 percent chance or greater of winning a contract. By weighting the importance of each answer and then calculating the end result, the firm can place its bets much more strategically and profitably. A new business rule would be that the business would never respond to an RFP unless it knew it had a 70 percent probability or higher of winning that contract. By reengineering the sales process in this way, a sales team can see its efficiency skyrocket since it will be spending less time and money on marketing and pitching proposals than on closing deals.

An insightful voice in this space is Tom Searcy, author of the book *Whale Hunting* (Wiley, 2008), in which he talks about how companies can effectively go after winning sales from big clients like Fortune 500 firms or the government by defining their business rules and the kinds of customers they want to engage. It's Tom's opinion that the RFP process is a waste of time if you don't know your odds of winning. He uses the analogy of playing Texas hold 'em, a version of poker where each player is dealt two cards, which they keep hidden. Five cards are then dealt face up one at a time. Bets are placed between each deal. What makes the game so interesting—and popular on TV—is that players are forced to make bets even though they only have access to a fraction of the information, two cards out of seven. They need to make an educated guess about what their opponent might be holding and their ability to beat that hand—just like when you're bidding on a contract.

What's fascinating is that the best players among the professionals and high-level amateurs who participate in tournaments like the World Series of Poker, for instance, fold their hands far more often than average players do. Those expert players realize that they need to have certain cards in their hand—a pair, an ace or two cards of the same suit, two adjacent cards—that will form the basis for an aggressive bet. And when these players have cards they like, they bet hard, sometimes even going all in. When they don't, they fold—every time.

Searcy says businesses can learn a lot from this strategy, which he calls your "Two Card Questions." Just as in poker, if you don't have the right conditions that indicate a high probability to win a contract, you should fold because the odds say that you're likely to lose whatever investment you make by bidding. If using predictive analytics can help you assess your odds of winning, even with two-sevenths of the total information, then you can more aggressively bet the money and resources needed to nail down that customer. The best firms push this thinking to the front of the funnel, targeting only those companies that have a very high probability of closing an order.

The Lazy CEO puts on the Engineer hat to engage in building systems. Systems that prevent mistakes, reduce work, and deliver high levels of performance for customers. Nothing is as frustrating for our Lazy CEO as redoing work because a system didn't deliver on the promise.

KEY POINTS

- The components of a business system are business rules, IT systems, training, and company values and culture.
- Nail down the business rules by making the implicit explicit.
- Measure to improve.
- Focus on applications to get the most out of your IT.
- Transform your approach to training: the human software.
- Use values to get the right decisions when there are no rules.
- Align all systems to the customer value proposition.
- Engineer "Wow!" by going beyond the expected.
- Cycle time is the single best measurement to show a good system.
- Streamline through "stapling" yourself to a customer experience.
- Refine your sales processes using predictive tools to determine what customers to pursue before you invest big money.

Chapter Six
THE PLAYER HAT

The best executive is one who has sense enough to pick good people to do what he wants done and self-restraint enough to keep from meddling with them while they do it.
—Theodore Roosevelt

Dick, a very successful CEO we know, tells this story from the early days in his company. Fresh out of the Navy, he was a phenomenal project manager. In fact, he was the best project manager in the company. He continued to perform this role as the business grew, justifying his decision because he was really good at it, projects ran smoothly, and he was teaching others how to be equally good. But one of his leaders came to him and said, "Dick, you may be our best project manager, but that's not what you are being paid to do." While he resisted it, this CEO finally realized that he was becoming a bottleneck for the talent in his business. He handed the project manager role over to others, which allowed Dick to take on the CEO role more completely. As it turned out, the people working for him grew into better project managers than he could have hoped—maybe even *better* than he was.

All respect to Teddy Roosevelt, but while most of the time a CEO should hire great people and get out of their way, there are times when he or she has to wear the Player hat. Wearing this hat might seem anathema to our Lazy CEO, but we advise him or her to go into Player mode to learn, with the specific objective of taking off the Player hat as soon as possible. As we saw in the case above,

Dick finally got out of Player mode and let his team perform, with excellent results.

Entrepreneurs tend to be people of action. While others plot, they act. As a result, these men and women often get a head start on the competition. While this bias for action can certainly result in their making mistakes because they didn't thoroughly think things out—a negative outcome—entrepreneurs nevertheless do get things done.

Most entrepreneurs also tend to excel in a particular area of their company: maybe it's sales, marketing, or even engineering. Perhaps it is their natural gift or they learned the skill in their first jobs. They know that if they use the same skills they used when they started the business and spend time on the tasks they're good at, they can make an impact, usually a big one. Doing that is how they can have some measure of how they are changing the outcome of their company in a direct way, like a smoothly run project in our example above. This is especially true when the company is in the early growth stage, that is, on the way to $15 million to $20 million in sales, when you can literally see the difference of your work. The revenue is the scorecard. It feels good to meet the company goals, improve year over year, and it's great for your ego.

This is what putting on your Player hat is all about. When you're in Player mode, you bring an incredible level of experience to the job, far beyond that of others in the company. You are like the ultimate A player in a role. You can make connections others can't, for instance, and you help bring the weight of the entire organization into deals in a way that no one else could. That's especially true in sales situations. Call it the "power of the business card," where a client sees that the CEO of the company is working on their deal, and they realize that they will get access to resources no typical salesperson has. Imagine how happy you'd be as a client if your project manager was also the CEO of the company!

But the trap here is that entrepreneurs can be lured into thinking that performing in Player mode is more important than it actually is, which can cause long-term damage to the business and result in lower growth. Let us illustrate.

Inc. CEO Project works with a CEO who runs a professional services company that works on business strategy with big-name brands like Dow Chemical and IBM. The CEO was a gifted salesperson; he was great at it and was responsible for landing many of the firm's largest clients. Consequently, he had a hard time removing himself from that role: in part because he got tremendous ego gratification from the sales results; in part because he struggled to find a replacement who could match his results; and in part because he wasn't sure where else he could add value to the enterprise.

This CEO decreased his sales involvement over time, but it took discipline and the cooperation of the organization. He first built a sales team of high performers and began to slowly back out. One of the ways he drove this kind of change was by billing the organization at the rate of $10,000 a day for his time. That meant the sales team thought twice before bringing him into any deal. Other sales leaders stepped up and performed. In fact, they helped drive record sales figures. Put another way, the more this CEO decreased his involvement, the better the results became because the other players in the organization were given more room to perform on their own. During that time, he was able to put on his Architect hat to shift his efforts to higher-value work, such as new products, strategic partnerships, and acquisitions. Remember, once you clear the kink in the hose, your job is to hand the hose to someone else in the organization.

LIMIT YOUR TIME AS A PLAYER

Although our case study CEO with superior salesmanship was spending up to 80 percent of his time working on landing clients, we've found that the most gifted Lazy CEOs actually spend only about

25 percent of their time wearing their Player hats once they are out of start-up mode. They pick one or two go-ahead projects a year in which they identify a constraint on the growth of the business. While it can be difficult for CEOs to put aside ego and possibly some of the tasks they truly enjoy working on, spending too much time in Player mode can actually have a serious negative impact on your company. Just recall our friend Dick, at the beginning of this chapter, who realized he was a bottleneck in the company he had founded.

What follows are three other adverse effects from wearing your Player hat for too long:

1. You face the risk of becoming a switchboard operator. If you are so central to your organization that everything goes through you, your productivity will be limited by how many hours you can invest in the job. That's why it's so common to hear that CEOs work eighty hours a week or more. But as the organization grows, they find they simply cannot work any more hours. They become like an octopus at a switchboard, and eventually they run out of capacity and the business stops making progress.

2. You also face the risk of failing to develop talent by being in Player mode excessively. If the people in your organization know you enjoy being involved in the sales process or in engineering, for example, it's natural for them to defer to you. But, by allowing this to happen, both you and your talented team risk seeing their skills stagnate. Ultimately, this means you can never sell the company for full value because any intelligent buyer will see that it won't run without you involved.

3. You focus on the urgent over the important issues in the

business. Remember that your managers are the ones who should concentrate on current business problems and delivering to clients. If you are not focused on the important longer-term issues, then no one in the organization is.

The key here, as with many things in life, is moderation. One reason you want to engage in Player mode is to stay connected to the business. When we interview CEOs, we ask them simple questions about key elements of their business like margin rates or product development timelines. All too often they simply don't know the answers. Sure, they know who has the answers, but it's essential for you as the CEO to have your finger on the pulse of your business as a whole. That's why occasionally jumping into a deal with a particular customer can be a smart move. James McNerney, the CEO of Boeing, did. He would engage in sales opportunities from time to time to get a sense of how his business was performing on the front lines. Granted, McNerney would wait until a really BIG deal (perhaps 10 percent of revenue or greater) came around, but he knew what his involvement meant.

McNerney also knew that the higher up in an organization you are—and the bigger the organization gets—the easier it is for information to get filtered before it reaches you. Key insights you need might be inadvertently edited out before they reach your desk or in-box. This is especially true about anything negative: No one lower in the food chain wants to be the one to deliver the bad news. Getting to the front of your organization can be particularly powerful in highly political organizations where individuals tend to push their own agendas ahead of the best interests of the organization as a whole. Getting on the front lines gives you a clarity that will prevent people from coloring the information they hand you because you will have firsthand knowledge already.

USE THE PLAYER HAT FOR META-WORK

One of the ways great CEOs get the most out of the time they spend in Player mode is by also focusing on meta-work, that is, thinking about the process rather than the actual work. This means that while in Player mode they are also wearing one of the other Lazy CEO hats: Architect, Coach, Engineer, and, primarily, Learner.

When you're in Player mode during a sales process, for example, you get to see your own talent in action, which is an essential part of the learning you will need when you are involved in Coach mode. If you're in Player mode related to, say, a product development process, you'll get the opportunity to assess if you have the right talent on your team capable of generating new ideas. You can also gain some valuable insight as an Architect or Engineer by assessing if there are ways to switch the business model to embrace subscription revenue or to redesign the process to make it better, faster, and cheaper, for example.

When you look at it this way, being in Player mode is actually akin to being in Learner mode, where you can constantly be asking the kinds of questions that are valuable to identifying and overcoming the key constraints in your business from a whole new perspective. The real opportunity, in other words, is the ability to learn and gather insight into other areas of your business.

Your goal when playing the Player role will be to have a clear pathway back into your CEO role as well as deep learning at the point of constraint. That means spending enough time with the Player hat on to learn what you need in order to get the most from going back to wearing the other hats. The Lazy CEO will then back out of Player mode by adding the needed talent and systems to a given area to improve its performance. For the CEO we met earlier who was helping his team with a major sale, he might come away knowing he needs to upgrade the team and change the offer to this kind of client to accelerate sales. That's a much greater payoff than landing one sale.

Putting on your Player hat is a valuable and effective use of your time as CEO, as long as you limit it to focusing on the following criteria:

- Work only on tasks that have a high impact on the organization.
- Make sure that you work with a team so you don't miss opportunities to assess or coach your talent.
- Be on the lookout for work in which you will learn something new from the tasks you are engaged in.
- Try to engage in Player mode only around the point of constraint for maximum learning and impact.

By focusing on tasks that both help remove constraints from your business and give you a new insight into the front lines of your operation, you, too, can be a winner when you have your Player hat on.

EMBRACING A DON'T-DO LIST

A key question every CEO faces is how they can get out of Player mode and spend more time in high-leverage roles like Architect, Coach, Engineer, and Learner. And the secret to getting there is the Don't-Do list. Everyone has a To-Do list. It helps us stay focused and organized. It's also an easy place to park things that we think we should be doing but don't have the time to tackle at that moment. There is nothing more satisfying than crossing something off your To-Do list; it gives us a little jolt of accomplishment and joy. Some people actually add to their list tasks they have already accomplished just so they can cross them off! Yet there is a tyranny in this practice because these tasks are usually the easy ones, the ones you would do anyway, such as checking and responding to your e-mail or updating your calendar. They are routine and generally not significant enough to impact results. They may be urgent, but they're not that important in the grand scheme of things.

Lazy CEOs also make To-Do lists, but they order the tasks beginning with those that will have the most economic impact to those that will have the least impact on their businesses. Then they make a key change. They draw a line across the page about halfway up the list and write on it "Don't-Do." Any task below the line should not be done, should be deferred, or should be delegated, as we detail below. While this might seem drastic—the items were added to the list for a reason, after all—the point is to get you to apply some strategy as you think about items that will have less economic impact on your firm. To help you with that process, we've listed the following 3D strategies for dealing with the items that typically fall under a CEO's Don't-Do list:

- The first strategy is to not **do** them. Make a decision that you are not going to spend time on any issues listed below the line. Hopefully the issues will go away or somehow be resolved without your involvement. In any case, you will not be taking action on these particular items at this time, or probably ever.
- The second strategy is to **defer**. This means you won't take action on a particular item for a while. Many times this delaying tactic will result in a reevaluation of the importance of the task (i.e., it ends up not being as critical as it once seemed). Occasionally someone from within your organization will step up and decide the task is important for him or her to complete. Other times, the situation will shift and the need for action

will go away. Deferring, of course, can be a hard choice for action-oriented leaders to make. But as we know, the bias for taking action is both a strength and a weakness for entrepreneurs. The truth is that waiting can work.
- The third and last strategy is to **delegate**. If an item is too important to defer, but it still doesn't rank in the top half of your personal list, it is a great one to delegate. Find the right person inside or outside the organization who can best accomplish this task, and then make it a point to assign it to that individual. People will generally be flattered that you, the CEO, have asked them to help. And what would seem like a normal task to you as the leader can seem like a real stretch assignment for an employee. This yields two benefits for you and the company: The task gets done, and you have developed an underling.

The Don't-Do list should be refreshed on a regular basis, perhaps monthly. Doing so will allow you to become more refined in what you work on and to shorten your personal To-Do list. And with regular maintenance, you can help make sure that you eliminate those pesky, unimportant issues that find their way onto your To-Do list while freeing you up to work on the most critical constraints facing your business.

THE 70 PERCENT RULE

How do you determine when it is the right time to delegate a task? Not knowing the answer to this question stops many CEOs from shifting tasks to their team. They wait until they feel that someone else is competent enough to complete the task as well as they can and thus doom themselves to owning that task for much longer than is necessary. Think about Dick, the project managing CEO you met as this chapter opened; this is exactly what stopped him from delegating the task. He didn't think anyone would be as good as he was at the job.

> Lazy CEOs use the 70 Percent Rule: If the person the CEO would like to assign to do the task is able to do it at least 70 percent as well as the CEO can, then the CEO should delegate it.

Lazy CEOs, on the other hand, use the 70 Percent Rule. Put simply, if the person the CEO would like to assign to do the task is able to do it at least 70 percent as well as the CEO can, then the CEO should delegate it. Is it frustrating that the task won't be done with the same level of perfection or perceived perfection that the CEO could achieve? Sure! But you need to let go of perfection. We all know it's easier said than done, but there is no place for perfection when it comes to delegation. The upside is you won't need to spend any time on the task—zero! The return on time you get for not working on the task is infinite, plus you gain that same time to invest in a higher-impact project.

Part of the delegation process involves knowing what you want to accomplish and then letting people know what is needed for your team members to get it done. Then it's time for perhaps the most difficult part of delegation: letting go and trusting that your team members will take the ball and run with it. This requires an understanding that they may do it in a way completely different from how you would do it. You may even be surprised to find that when you give your team members a little leeway, they discover new—and better—ways to do things.

Clearly some tasks require a 100 percent performance level. You will choose not to delegate these tasks. You could, however, transfer them to someone on your team, knowing that the team member will likely need extensive support and training. One-on-one oversight may also be required. One company we work with was doing a major debt offer. The CFO had never been involved in a transaction of this size and complexity, yet it had to go right. The CEO delegated the project but kept in close contact with the CFO throughout the process. Ultimately, the financing was successful. And the larger impact from the investment of time the CEO made in the CFO on this project was that the CFO carried off the next two refinancing projects without assistance. Delegation on critical projects generally will require more coaching than will less critical ones.

One important point to remember is that if you delegate a task fully, you shouldn't try to coach the delegate to get back that 30 percent difference. While delegation doesn't mean you are no longer responsible, that doesn't mean you should pull the project off the desk of the person you assigned the task the minute things get tough. This is how people learn, and the good ones will have a few sleepless nights as they make sure that everything does go right. If you try to coach the difference in performance between how you would handle the task and how it is being handled, you take away the other person's ownership, meaning you never really delegated it. People will sense this. Before you know it, that task will be back on your desk permanently.

When it comes to effective delegation, you need to communicate clearly, concisely, and consistently, and you also need to make sure that each team member has access to the same information. If you used certain business rules or data sources to successfully execute a project, then you have to make these available. Unfortunately, this can mean financial data or other private information you'd rather not share. The loss of critical data is outweighed, however, by your ability to get it off your desk and fully delegate the task.

Trust is one of the most important factors when it comes to delegation, and it goes both ways. You need to trust that your team members will complete the work they are responsible for, and your team members need to trust that you are giving them all of the information they need to do the work. You will be available to back them up when necessary. Lazy CEOs have learned the art of sitting on their hands and biting their lips while a team member does a task completely differently but with 70 percent—or higher—results. Obviously, if they ask for coaching, you have a free pass to give feedback without taking away ownership; but, be judicious in the feedback—no essays on how to do it your way.

> Lazy CEOs have learned the art of sitting on their hands and biting their lips while a team member does a task completely differently but with 70 percent—or higher—results.

No Monday morning quarterbacking, either. We've all had the experience of walking into a manager's office, smiling and proud of our recent accomplishment, only to get a lesson on what we "should" have done differently. If you, as a CEO, do this, you will suck the energy, passion, and ownership right out of the new task owner, who will simply defer to you—and you will never really rid yourself of the task. Your goal is to delegate, recapture time for higher-level tasks, develop the employee, and achieve success.

Effective delegation can be the answer, particularly for time-challenged small-business owners who are struggling to find the time to grow their businesses. And when you take measures to set yourself up for an effective delegation process, you're not only giving yourself time to focus on your most vital business activities, but also alleviating some of the pressure of always doing everything yourself.

When you are considering whether or not to delegate a task, ask yourself, "Can my staff do it 70 percent as well as I would?" If so, it is time to let it go!

THE 80 PERCENT RULE FOR FEEDBACK

Many entrepreneurs have high standards when it comes to performance. You might even call them perfectionists. That means they'll often have a lot of feedback and input anytime someone asks their opinion on something. In fact, for many it's what they live for. They love problem solving. Some even create problems to solve, but that is for another book.

Being too free with your feedback comes with a steep price, though. There are times when keeping your mouth shut as a CEO can be the wisest strategy. That's where the 80 Percent Rule comes into play. If your employees are 80 percent right and they own the task wholly, then be quiet unless asked.

Let's say you have an employee ask you for some feedback on a project he or she is running. Right off the bat, you immediately see some areas that could be better run. Fundamentally the person is headed in the right direction, has it at least 80 percent right, and 100 percent owns the outcome. You can feel the passion. The danger in opening your mouth and offering significant feedback and direction is that once you do, you've taken ownership of that project. It becomes your work, and you will cause your employee to lose a sense of ownership over the project.

If a project is mission critical to the survival of the firm, all bets are off. But for anything less sensitive, if a project is 80 percent on target, then you should keep your mouth shut. You might think this conflicts with the 70 Percent Rule, but when initially delegating something, you have the right to offer coaching to orient someone and get their performance higher than 70 percent good enough. Or, rather, tell your employee something like, "Great job! Now jump on it and execute on the rest of it!" That man or woman will leave, proud and ready to push even harder.

Sure, you could have helped that employee get to the point where the outcome met 100 percent of your expectations, but you'd lose his or her heart and soul in the process. You'd rather have an employee who is 100 percent committed to a project that is only 80 percent of the way there than have someone only 80 percent committed to something you thought was 100 percent on target. See the distinction?

Another strategy to use when a subordinate asks for feedback is to ask, in turn, "Is that the best you can do?" Many times, this question alone is enough to incent really driven employees to say they will take another crack at making it better. The employee will still do all the work, which means remaining engaged and retaining a sense of ownership.

If an employee says yes, that was his or her best effort, and it was still 80 percent good enough, then you say, "Great job!" and run with it. This is particularly true for a project that will not damage the business if it isn't perfect. The reason most delegated employees think they are on task is because they haven't yet learned enough to understand a higher standard. Insightful employees, however, will analyze their performance and strive to do better the next time. So, less than perfect work doesn't stay at that level for long. We've all said after a first attempt at something that we can do better the second time around.

We've heard a story about an employee who sent a project he had completed to his leader and then came to discuss it. The leader asked if it was the best he could do. The employee admitted he could probably do better and asked if he could work on it a bit more. He came back a week later. Again, the leader asked, "Is this the best you can do?" The employee admitted that he could improve a few areas, and he made those changes. The third time he brought the project to the leader, he said it was the best work he could do. The leader replied, "Then I'll read it now." While the story feels a little manipulative, the employee continued to own the project and ultimately did the best work he was capable of without the leader diving in to help or taking ownership.

It will always be more valuable for your employees to own their work. Ownership is the true foundation for building and retaining an engaged workforce.

WEAR YOUR PLAYER HAT SPARINGLY

When most CEOs find their company getting into some kind of bind, they jump in to help resolve the issue. We call this going into Player Mode. "I'm just helping out for now," a CEO might tell himself. "I'll bring in someone else later." Unfortunately, CEOs with this mindset will usually get psychic rewards from the work and find it hard to exit if they are anxious to jump into something. The impact of the good job is another issue because they will find it hard to get someone their equal in the area.

But the great and Lazy CEOs out there rarely enter into Player Mode; rather, their first move is to find someone else to do the work. They are very intentional about engaging the organization. That's why great CEOs are lazy. Consider what that means in this context. Of course great CEOs work hard, but the hard work they do is in finding, recruiting, and engaging the best people to get the task at hand done as well as they can.

Think back to your high school reading list and recall the story of Tom Sawyer and how he found a way to recruit his friends to help him paint a fence for his aunt. Tom found a way to make the job sound so exciting that he even got his friends *to pay him* for the privilege of doing it!

Now, we are not advocating using sleight of hand in tackling the issues at your workplace. What we are emphasizing, however, is that as soon as you, as CEO, engage in Player mode, you lose your ability to recruit other people to get the work done because you are busy.

This notion is very counterintuitive. For many of us, we began our working lives at the age of fourteen or sixteen, cutting lawns or bussing tables or the like. We have worked our whole lives. The idea of not working is somehow offensive to our sense of an internal work ethic. But being "lazy" in this case is all about working smarter, not harder.

> Some CEOs get "lazier" the worse things get in the sense that they work harder to get the right people involved in solving the problem, while personally detaching themselves from the situation as much as they can to remain objective.

Case in point: We recently met up with the CEO of a professional services company. The top priority for his firm was growing its client base. In fact, they planned to double it in a year. The CEO mentioned how he planned to work harder to help the firm meet its goals. We asked him what he meant. After all, he couldn't realistically work twice as hard as he was already, right? And how feasible was it that he could help the company literally double the rate at which it closed new deals? The only option on the table that might work was to get more people involved in the process. What he needed to do was to get lazy. He needed to do less customer and sales work and do more recruiting of people who could do that work for the company instead.

There will always be times where, when the stuff really hits the proverbial fan, you, as CEO, might have to step in to do some actual "work" deep in Player mode. But the great CEOs will make that their fourth or fifth option. In fact, some CEOs get "lazier" the worse things get, in the sense that they work harder to get the right people involved in solving the problem while personally detaching themselves from the situation as much as they can to remain objective. Not only is that a great way to ensure that the right person is doing the job, it's also a great empowerment and team-building approach. Rather than you as CEO parachuting in to save the day, your team will begin to learn that they are the ones who are trusted to save things for themselves. No one is coming to save them. That's powerful stuff.

Unless you are really good at what needs to be done, or truly enjoy it, you're better off with the lazy solution. Even Steve Jobs, who in some ways was the epitome of the micromanager, really stuck with just a few things he cared about, like the design and look and feel of the products. You didn't hear about him getting wrapped up in solving operational issues or things dealing with production and manufacturing. He wasn't designing circuit boards. He let the people who were pros at those tasks solve their own issues.

So the moral of the story, as you might have guessed by now, is that being lazy pays off for the best CEOs out there. You might ask yourself how your business could benefit if you started doing less and getting lazy.

KEY POINTS

- Spend only 25 percent of your time in Player mode.
- Don the Player hat for meta-work.
- Embrace a Don't-Do list.
- Use the 70 Percent Rule for delegation.
- Use the 80 Percent Rule for feedback.
- Be Tom Sawyer Lazy and find excellent people to do the work.

CONCLUSION

*Executive ability is deciding quickly and
getting somebody else to do the work.*
—Earl Nightingale

If we had to summarize the approach of the Lazy CEO in a couple of words, they would be *focus* and *leverage*. The entire diagnostic process of determining the point of constraint in your business is about finding the right area to focus your time on. Being lazy, you really don't want to start working hard without a clear understanding of the potential impact of your time. Sometimes this is crystal clear, and the diagnostic step can be done quickly. Other times, significant effort is required to untangle the problem and get to the very root. To outsiders this might not look like real work, and for entrepreneurs with a bias for action, it can be painful. The legendary business leader Earl Nightingale nicely summarizes the whole approach: Decide what needs to be done and find someone else to do it.

Lazy CEOs remember the scene in *Alice's Adventures in Wonderland* when Alice meets the Cheshire Cat.

> "Cheshire Puss," she began, rather timidly, as she did not at all know whether it would like the name: however, it only grinned a little wider. "Come, it's pleased so far," thought Alice, and she went on. "Would you tell me, please, which way I ought to go from here?"

> "That depends a good deal on where you want to get to," said the Cat.
>
> "I don't much care where—" said Alice.
>
> "Then it doesn't matter which way you go," said the Cat.
>
> "—so long as I get *somewhere*," Alice added as an explanation.
>
> "Oh, you're sure to do that," said the Cat, "if you only walk long enough."

Hardworking and misguided CEOs have the same logic. It's not actually critical that they get clear on where they are going, as long as they work hard enough. If they do that they are sure to get somewhere.

Think back to the analogy we used at the start of the book, the kinked hose. If you spend the time to determine where the kink is in the hose, rather than just tugging on it hoping the kink will come out, it is well worth your time—if you are lazy. Once that kink is identified, it is clear that you should focus on removing it. The same is true in your business. Lazy CEOs give as much of their time as possible—usually between 30 and 50 percent—specifically to the task of removing the constraint in the business. This laser-focus on the critical issue provides a real and, over time, compounding impact.

Once the kink in the hose, the point of constraint in the business, is identified, our hardworking CEOs will dive into the problem up to their elbows until the issue is resolved. This is not the approach of Lazy CEOs. Rather, they think about engaging the point of constraint in a leveraged way. They want to unkink the hose, but in a way that builds organizational capacity and pays them back for the investment of their time. They do this by donning one of the five hats: Learner, Architect, Coach, Engineer, or Player.

Lazy CEOs have a pretty simple game plan. Find the point of constraint that has the highest economic impact, engage in fixing the constraint in a high-leverage way that builds organizational ability, and repeat. Now that you know, we hope you look at your business differently, work less, and get great results. Now get busy being lazy!

ACKNOWLEDGMENTS

I wanted to acknowledge a number of people who directly contributed to the creation of this book: Henry Schleckser, Jim Haudan, Dave Warren, Dick Stieglitz, Kirk Aubry, Neal Rothermel, Jim Parm, Darren Dahl, Lari Bishop, Jay Hodges, Alex Head, Linda O'Doughda, Patrick Hainault, Pam Singleton, and RJ Nicolosi. Your assistance has been invaluable and is deeply appreciated. A number of the concepts in this book were developed by and in conjunction with Mark Helow and I thank him for his important contributions.

INDEX

A
ADT Corporation, 66, 67
Alice's Adventures in Wonderland, 177
Alignment with strategic advantage, 23–24
Amazon, 88
American Express, 63
Architect hat, 2, 11–12, 26, 27, 57–92, 161
    in assessing business, 14–18
    business models in, 58–62
    remodeling the business, 62–92;
        capital velocity in, 58, 80–85;
        mafia offer in, 58, 85–88;
        moat building in, 58, 62–65;
        recurring revenue in, 65–80;
        simple is hard in, 58, 89–91
Attitude, making a shift in your, 34–36
Autonomy, 114
Avnet, 83

B
Back office, 138
Baekeland, Leon, 14
Basic Recurring Revenue, 69
Beane, Billy, 94
Best Buy, 76
Black pool, 60
Blockbuster, 67
Board
    of advisors, 46
    building a, 46–50
    CEO coaching and role of, 51–55
    changes in composition of, 50
    of directors, 46
    insight on, 47
    money role on, 47–48
    oversight on, 46–47
    skills matrix for, 49–50
    utilizing social and business networks, 48–49
Boeing, 163
Bootstrap start-up, 98–99
Boy Scouts, Scout Law of, 142–143
Brando, Marlon, 86
The Breakthrough Company (McFarland), 37–38, 132
Brief (McCormack), 89
Buffett, Warren, 62–63, 65
Bundling, in adding recurring revenue, 78
Business
    adding recurring revenue to your, 73–75
    customers in funding, 82
    defined, 131
    suppliers in funding, 83
Business assessment, 13–25
    architect hat in, 14–18
    coach hat in, 19–21
    engineer hat in, 21–24
    learner hat in, 13–14
    player hat in, 24–25
Business model problems, 14–18
Business models, 58–62
    capital velocity in, 58, 80–85
    mafia offer in, 58, 85–88
    moat building in, 58, 62–65

recurring revenue in, 58, 65–80
simple is hard in, 58, 89–91
Business rules, 135–137, 142
Business system (see also Engineer hat)
   business rules in, 135–137
   company values and culture in, 142–143
   information technology in, 137–140
   training in, 140–142
Businessweek, 2

C

Can't-Do list, 5
Capital, cost of, 18
Capital employment, low return on, 17–18
Capital intensity, 15–16, 110
Capital velocity, 58, 80–85
   calculating, 81–82
   choosing customers who pay quickly, 82–83
   in controlling growth rate, 84
   customers in funding business, 82
   negotiating free consigned inventory, 83–84
   suppliers in funding of business, 83
Cards, playing right, 154–156
Cash, power of, 80
Catastrophic events, 49
CEO peer groups, 38–39, 54
CEOs
   primary mission of, 6–8
   using position to develop potential leaders, 118
CFO, 169
   uncovering errors made by, 19
Chief talent officers, acquisition of top performers and, 97–105
Coach hat, 2, 12, 26, 27, 93–129
   in assessing business, 19–21
   cultivating top performers as next generation of leaders, 115–122
   dealing with or divesting yourself of underperformers, 122–126
   evaluating talent and, 105–110
   motivating top performers, 111–115
   onboarding new hires, 110–111
   reinforcing the culture, 126–128
Coaching
   offering, for improvement, 123
   role of the board and, 51–55
Commitment(s)
   to learning, 20
   missed, 22
   to performance, 20
Company, acquiring top performers, 97–105
Company flow rate, 6
Company growth
   bootstrap start-up and, 98–99
   middle-growth stage and, 100–102
   well-funded start-up and, 99–100
Company values and culture, 142–143
Complexity of mental processing (CMP), 35–36, 44
ConstantContact, 71–72
Constraint(s)
   as controllable, 10–12
   identifying point of, 5–29
Context, 138
Contracted Recurring Revenue, 69–71
Counterintuitive ideas, 39–40, 83
Crosby, Phil, 93
Crowning the company, 132
Culture, reinforcing the, 126–128
Customer relationship management (CRM), 70, 71
Customers
   choosing those who pay quickly, 82–83
   in funding business, 82
Cycle time, improving, 23

D

DailyPuppy.com, 58

Data-based coaching, 53
Data moat, 63–64
Data transfer moat, 70
Dealing with Darwin (Moore), 138
Defects, in Toyota Production System (TPS), 22–23, 151
Deferral strategy, 166–167
Delegating, 167
Deloitte Fast 50, 2
Demand Media, 58, 59–60
Direct mail companies, 152–153
The Discipline of Market Leaders (Tracy and Wiersema), 144
Don't do list, embracing a, 165–167
Dow Chemical, 161
Drive (Pink), 114–115
DropBox, 72
Dynamic pricing, 41

E
eBay, 72
EBITDA, 60, 113
EBITDA level, 113
Education, 116–117, 124
　in embracing learning opportunities, 119
　executive, 52
　lifelong learning and, 33–34
　one-on-one coaching and, 52–53
　training and, 77, 140–142
Ego gratification, 161
eHarmony, 72–73
80 percent rule for feedback, 171–173
Employees
　assessment of, 107–110
　covering for low-performing, 19
　need to cover for terminated, 25
　not rehiring, 19–20
Employee talent, 12
　problems with, 19–21
The E Myth (Gerber), 131–132
Energy, ideas and, 20–21
Engineer hat, 2, 12, 26, 28, 131–157, 149
　aligning systems to value proposition, 143–145
　in assessing business, 21–24
　elements of a business system, 135–143; focusing on company values and culture, 142–143; information technology, 137–140; nailing down business rules, 135–137; training, 140–142
　engineering "wow," 145–146
　improving and measuring, 133–134
　measuring to improve, 152–153
　picking up speed, 148–149
　playing your cards right, 154–156
　scaling up, 146–148
　speed in product development, 153–154
　streamlining through stapling, 150–152
Enterprise car rental, 146
Enterprise resource planning (ERP) system, 71
Entrepreneurs
　as builders, 57
　innate self-confidence in, 46
　as people of action, 160
　in taking fresh look, 58
Equity, 113
Ernst & Young Entrepreneuer of the Year, 2
Ethernet, 64
Example, setting an, 24–25
Exclusive Resorts, 85
Executive education, 52
Exit time, 125–126
Expected return on capital, 17–18
External rewards, 112–113

F
FedEx, 126–127
Feedback, 80 percent rule for, 171–173
Financial data, 134

Financing, in adding recurring revenue, 77–78
Focus, 177
Fontane, Johnny, 86
Forbes, 2
Ford Motor Co., 67
The Fountainhead (Rand), 57–58
Four Seasons Hotel, 139, 143

G

Game of Thrones, 62
GardenGuides.com, 58
Garden hose analogy, 7–8, 178
Gates, Bill, 1
GE, 73–74, 80
Gerber, Michael, 131–132
The Godfather, 86
Golden Rolodex, 48–49
Goldratt, Eliyahu, 5, 6–7, 15, 86
GolfLink.com, 58
Google ads, 59
Great CEOs, skills of, 2
Great Recession, 136
Gross margin, 85
    low, 16
Groupon, 72
Growth rate, capital velocity in controlling, 84

H

Healthcare, 32
Heath, Chip, 126
Heath, Dan, 126
Hertz, 146
Heskett, James L., 133
High tech, 32
Hires, onboarding new, 110–111
Homes of Hope, 136
Hospitality companies, 144
Hulu, 88
Human resource management (HRM) system, 71
Humility, need for, 34

I

IBM, 161
Ideas
    counterintuitive, 39–40, 83
    energy and, 20–21
    inflow off, 34
    outflow of, 34
    sleep time in generating, 42–43
Immersion, 37
Improvement
    coaching for, 123
    measurement and, 133–135
Inc. CEO Project, 1, 11, 36–37, 81, 93, 161, 196
Inc. magazine, 2
Industries, learning from other, 39–41
Inflow, of ideas, 34
Information technology, 137–140
Insight, 47
Inspirato, 85
Insurance policies, in adding recurring revenue, 76
Intellectual property, 64
Intellectual property moat, 64
Internal rewards, 113–115
Interviewing, 102–103
    team, 103–104
Inventory
    negotiating free consigned, 83–84
    in Toyota Production System (TPS), 22–23, 151
Investing, in organizational learning, 43–44
Issues, awareness of, 123

J

Jaques, Elliott, 35
JDE, 71
Job shrinkage, 124
Jones, Thomas O., 133

K

Kansas City Royals, 96
Kissinger, Henry, 36

L

Lazy CEOs, 2–3
   business models for, 58–62, 90–91
   dealing with time constraints, 9–10
   game plan of, 178–179
   garden hose analogy for, 7–8
   job of, 93
   love for recurring revenue, 66
   making of hard decisions and, 2
   moat building and, 62–65
   need to make hard choices, 2
   playing favorites with time, 8
   as team member, 24
   time allocation and, 161–162

Leaders
   acknowledgment off, 2
   cultivating top performers as next generation of, 115–122
   education of, 116–117
   increasing breadth of, 117
   increasing scope of, 117
   leveraged roles of, 2–3, 6
   mentoring, 117–118

Learner hat, 2, 11, 26, 27, 28, 31–56, 149
   in assessing business, 13–14
   attitude shifts in, 34–36
   board skills matrix and, 49–50
   building a board, 46–50
   catastrophic event in, 49
   CEO coaching and the role of the board, 51–55
   executive education in, 52, 55
   golden rolodex in, 48–49
   insight in, 47
   investing in organizational learning, 43–44
   learning from other industries, 39–41
   lifelong learning in, 33–34
   making time to travel, 41
   modeling of learning for organization, 32–33
   money in, 47–48
   need in, 51–52
   networking group in, 38–39, 55
   one-on-one coaching and, 52–53, 55
   oversight in, 46–47
   peer groups in, 37–39, 55
   as pivotal role, 31
   player mode in, 36–37
   preparing to learn, 42–43
   reading as a priority, 41–42
   strategic consultation in, 54, 55

Learning
   commitment to, 20
   embracing opportunities for, 119
   identifying best way of, 25
   lifelong, 33–34
   modeling, for your organization, 32–33
   preparing for, 42–43

Lettres provinciales (Pascal), 89
Leverage, 2–3, 177
Lewis, Michael, 94
Lifelong learning, 33–34
Lifetime value of customer, 66
LinkedIn, 72, 73
LiquidNet, 60, 73
Los Angeles Dodgers, 96
Loveman, Gary W., 133

M

Macy's, 63
Made to Stick (Heath and Heath), 126
Mafia Offer, 15, 58, 85–88, 144, 154
Maintenance contracts, in adding recurring revenue, 76–77
Mastery, 114–115
The Matrix, 36
Maxwell, John C., 131
McCormack, Joseph, 89
McDonald's, 22, 82
McFarland, Keith, 37–38, 132
McNerrney, James, 163
Measurement, improvement and, 133–135

Mentoring, 117–118
Mergers and acquisitions, 47–48
Merlin International, 74–75, 80
Meta-work, using player hat for, 164–165
Metcalfe, Robert, 64
Metrics, 13
Microsoft Office, 71
Middle-growth stage, 100–102
Middle management, lack of, 116
Minimum viable product (MVP), 153–154
Mistakes, fear of making, 46
Moat building, 58, 62–65
    data moat in, 63–64
    intellectual property moat, 64
    network moat, 64
    speed moat, 65
    switching-cost moat, 64–65
    talent moat, 65
Momentum, lack of, 15
Money, 47–48
Moneyball (Lewis), 94
Moore, Geoffrey, 138
Motel 6, 88
Motion, in Toyota Production System (TPS), 22–23, 151

N

NeQoS, 103, 111
Netflix, 67, 87–88
Networked Recurring Revenue, 72–73
Networking group, distinguishing peer group from, 38–39
Network moat, 64
New York Yankees, 96
Nightingale, Earl, 177
Nordstrom, 134–135

O

Oakland As, 94, 96
Office 360, 71
Office 2013, 71
One-on-one coaching, 52–53
Online dating services, 72–73

Oracle, 71
    acquisition of JDE, Siebel, and PeopleSoft, 71
Organizational learning, making investing in, 43–44
Organization, modeling learning for, 32–33
Outflow, of ideas, 34
Outsourced organization, 138
Over-clubbing, 147
Over-hiring, 104–105
Over-processing, in Toyota Production System (TPS), 22–23, 151
Over-production, in Toyota Production System (TPS), 22–23, 151
Oversight, 46–47
Overspraying, 154–155

P

Pascal, Blaise, 89
Pay, performance-based, 120–121
Peanut buttering, 8, 9
Peer group
    distinguishing from networking group, 38–39
    joining a, 37–38
PeopleSoft, 71
Performance-based pay, 120–121
Performance, commitment to, 20
Performers
    cultivating top, as next generation of leaders, 115–122
    motivating top, 111–115
Phantom stock, 113
Phelps, David, 74–75, 80
Philips Corporation, 68
Pink, Daniel, 114–115
Player hat, 2, 12, 26, 28, 159–175
    in assessing business, 24–25
    80 percent rule for feedback, 171–173
    embracing a don't-do list, 165–167
    limiting time as player, 161–163

70 percent rule, 167–170
  using, for meta-work, 164–165
  wearing sparingly, 173–175
Player, limiting time as a, 161–163
Player mode, going into, 36–37
Position, changing the, 124–125
Prior behavior, looking at, 44
Problem solving, 6
Procter & Gamble, 82
Product development, speed in, 153–154
Professional facilitators, 38
Profitability, 13
  low, 16–17
Profit center, 75
Proprietary content, 88
Publishers Clearing House, 153
Purpose, 114

Q
QUALCOMM, 64
Quickbooks, 147

R
Rand, Ayn, 57–58
Rangan, V. Kasturi, 150
Reading, making a priority, 41–42
Recurring revenue, 58, 65–80
  adding to your business, 73–75
  basic, 69
  bundling in, 78
  contracted, 69–71
  financing in, 77–78
  as growth strategy, 66–68
  maintenance contracts in, 76–77
  networked, 72–73
  repeat revenue as, 68–69
  sequential and, 71–72
  service in, 75–76
  shifting in, 78–80
  training in, 77
Remodeling the business, see Architect hat
Repeat Revenue, 68–69
Request for proposal (RFP), 155

Revenue, 13
  low recurring, 17
Reviews, 119–120
Rewards, 119–120
  external, 112–113
  internal, 113–115
Risk factors
  identifying, 13
  resolving, 27
Ritz-Carlton, 44, 142
ROAR (recruitment, orientation, activation, and retention), 110
Rolex, 112
Roosevelt, Theodore, 159
Root cause, identifying, 9

S
Salesforce.com, 70
Sasser, W. Earl, Jr., 133
Scaffolding, 37–38
Scaling up, 146–148
Schleckser, Jim, 196
Schlesinger, Leonard A., 133
Scout Law of the Boy Scouts, 142–143
Searcy, Tom, 155–156
Self-confidence, 46
Sequential and Recurring Revenue, 71–72
Service, in adding recurring revenue, 75–76
Service-profit chain, 133
70 percent rule, 167–170
Shapiro, Benson P., 150
Shifting, in adding recurring revenue, 78–80
Siebel, 71
Simple is hard strategy, 58, 89–91
Sleep time, 42–43
Smart, Brad, 105
Smart, Geoff, 105
Sourcing, 102–103
Southwest Airlines, 135
Speed
  picking up, 148–149

in product development, 153–154
Speed moat, 65
Stapling, streamlining through, 150–152
Start, knowing where, 13–14
Start-up
    bootstrap, 98–99
    well-funded, 99–100
S.T.E.W., 141
Stew Leonard's, 141–142
Strategic advantage, alignment with, 23–24
Strategic consultation, 54
Strategies, 31
Streamlining, through stapling, 150–152
Super 8, 88
Superstars, need to hire, 21–22
Suppliers, in funding business, 83
Sviokla, John, 150
Switching-cost moat, 64–65

T

Taco Bell, 132–133
Tactics, 31
Talent, evaluating, 105–110
Talent moat, 65
Team
    commitment to learning, 20
    commitment to performance, 20
    in interviewing, 103–104
    need to help, 24
Theory of Constraints, 6
3Com, 64
3M, 144
360-degree reviews, 53
Time
    limiting as a player, 161–163
    in Toyota Production System (TPS), 22–23, 151
Time allocation, error of uniform, 8–10
Timeliness, predictable, 22
To-do list, 165, 166
Top executive development, 51–52
Topgrading (How to Hire, Coach, and Keep A Players) (Smart and Smart), 105
Toyota Production System (TPS), 22–23, 151
    defects in, 22, 151
    inventory in, 22, 151
    motion in, 22, 151
    over-processing in, 22, 151
    over-production in, 22, 151
    time in, 22, 151
    waiting in, 22, 151
Trails.com, 58, 59
Training, 140–142
    in adding recurring revenue, 77
Trammell, Joel, 103, 104, 111
Travel, making time to, 41
Treacy, Michael, 144
Trust, 169–170
Two Card Questions, 156

U

Underperformers, dealing with or divesting yourself of, 122–126
U.S. military, 44

V

Value proposition, 12
Verizon, 44

W

Waiting, in Toyota Production System (TPS), 22–23, 151
Waitley, Denis, 31–32

Walmart, 82
Warranty policies, in adding recurring revenue, 76
Welch, Jack, 73–74, 80, 138
Well-funded start-up, 99–100
Whale Hunting (Searcy), 155
Wiersema, Fred, 144
World Series of Poker, 156

Y
Youth With A Mission, 136

Z
Zero inventory, 82

ABOUT THE AUTHOR

Jim Schleckser is the CEO of the Inc. CEO Project and helps leaders grow companies. Jim Schleckser is the CEO of the Inc. CEO Project, an organization that builds peer groups and advises high performing CEOs. They specialize in helping growth companies scale up their business models, talent, processes, and systems. Jim and his team advise hundreds of CEOs of high-growth companies around the country to help them sustain their success.

With thirty years of leadership in business strategy, technology businesses, process improvement, organizational development, mergers and acquisitions, engineering, sales, and marketing, Jim brings to the table experience in leading global organizations in both public and private environments across many functional areas. He has done business in more than twenty-six countries.

As a Lazy CEO, he also finds time to be a soccer player, Cross Fitter, prolific reader, and outdoorsman. He resides in Potomac, Maryland.

He can be reached at jimschleckser@IncCEOProject.com.